"*Brutalities* is electric with insight, riveted by its commitments to love and bewilderment, to bearing witness—and utterly propulsive in its explorations of compulsion, tenderness, caregiving, and desire. Margo Steines sees the world fiercely and freshly, with a rapt and nuanced gaze utterly her own. Imagine journeying to the center of the earth, except the earth is a human body—full of wanting and haunting—and the journey is just harrowing and glorious enough to do justice to the work and wonder of being alive."

—Leslie Jamison, author of *Make It Scream, Make It Burn* and *The Empathy Exams*

"*Brutalities* is a perfect book. Reading it felt like consuming something designed precisely for me and of course, I won't be alone in this—that is the genius of great works of art: they reach our deepest interiors by naming the unspoken ordinary, the things we fear seeing or being seen as. There is nothing ordinary about this book, however. It is a brainy, elegant, erotic, brutal, funny, hypnotic achievement by an author obsessed with the far reaches of what it means to live in a body, and how some kinds of love look like violence while others can be medicine. It has made a devotee of me; I'll read anything Margo Steines ever writes."

—Melissa Febos, author of *Girlhood* and *Body Work*

"This book circles around the simple fact that each of us is capable of change. It does not matter where we've been or what we've done or what's been done to us, change is always possible. Margo Steines, through what some might call *grace*, has emerged from a (perhaps) chosen darkness, to focus all her wild energies into these pages. To get here she had to descend into realms you might find disturbing, but trust that if you descend with her (the trip is exhilarating) you too will emerge, also changed. This book is an amazing feat, Steines has crafted something truly lovely, and it's her writing that makes it sing."

—Nick Flynn, author of *This Is the Night Our House Will Catch Fire* and *Another Bullshit Night in Suck City*

"Margo Steines is a radical writer and also a slyly hilarious one. She goes places most of us dare not go and comes back with surprising truths that tell us as much about us as they do about her. This is the trick of great self-writing, to understand just how capacious the self can be and how porous with the wildnesses of the world. Steines's writing is alive, weird, dark, and electric."

—Ander Monson, author of *Predator: A Memoir, a Movie, an Obsession* and *The Gnome Stories*

BRUTALITIES

a love story

MARGO STEINES

W. W. NORTON & COMPANY
Celebrating a Century of Independent Publishing

For information about permission to reproduce selections from this book, write to
Permissions, W. W. Norton & Company, Inc., 500 Fifth Avenue, New York, NY 10110

For information about special discounts for bulk purchases, please contact
W. W. Norton Special Sales at specialsales@wwnorton.com or 800-233-4830

Manufacturing by Lakeside Book Company
Book design by Chris Welch
Production manager: Lauren Abbate

ISBN 978-1-324-05087-2

W. W. Norton & Company, Inc., 500 Fifth Avenue, New York, N.Y. 10110
www.wwnorton.com

W. W. Norton & Company Ltd., 15 Carlisle Street, London W1D 3BS

1 2 3 4 5 6 7 8 9 0

For N

Author's Note

This book deals with many distressing topics that may be difficult to read about. They were difficult in the living, too. Because I have no way of predicting who might be traumatized by which parts, I cannot offer a meaningfully specific content warning beyond saying this is a difficult book. It is always a good idea to care for your emotional state; please consider this note a reminder to do so.

Two true things:

1. I wrote this book with tremendous care to tell the truth to the best of my ability. There are no composite characters or events. I changed some names and I compressed time to tell a story that spans years.
2. The human memory is not a recording device. My memory and experience are as fallible and subjective as anyone's, meaning

they are subject to the influences of time, trauma, drugs, and other mind-altering forces. If you find yourself in the pages of this book and your experience differs from mine—you may be as correct as I am. Such is the nature of memory.

"Do you not see how necessary a World of Pains and troubles is to school an Intelligence and make it a soul? A Place where the heart must feel and suffer in a thousand diverse ways!"

—JOHN KEATS, *Selected Letters*

Contents

BRUTALITIES

EVERYTHING IS CONTAGIOUS

A pile of failed paper cranes is accumulating in my lap. They are shiny gold and marked by wrong folds, off angles, hesitant bend marks. I had thought, when I ordered the sheaf of yellow gold paper on the internet, that I would become excellent at origami and I would make a paper crane for each day I was quarantined. I thought I would end up with a fun pile of glinting birds, and it would be like meditating. I thought I would find some peace. Instead, I have burned through much of my paper with only this pile of crumples to show for it.

I am thirty-seven, pregnant, in love, and effectively locked in my apartment. In April the temperature nears the record high in Tucson, the southern Arizona desert town that has become my home. I did not intend to land in the Southwest—I was just stopping by for a few years to earn a graduate degree before heading back to Hawai'i, where I had settled. And yet, now I live here, nestled between the Catalina, Tortolita, Santa Rita, and Rincon mountain ranges, on a dusty alluvial plain tucked into great expanses of red voters and stabby cacti and desert creatures that hiss and howl at night.

On my couch sits my reason for staying here. His hair, nearly black, curls around his ears as he squints to read something on his phone screen. N: strong and gentle and wise, the person I spent so many years of my life stumbling around looking for. Our baby will be born at the end of the summer, into three-digit temperatures and monsoon rains.

My apartment is a collection of white objects nesting inside more white: white sheetrock living room, bedroom, and bathroom containing white modular shelves, white appliances, white table, white chairs. I keep the gauzy white curtains pulled tight against the Arizona sun at all times of the day. I keep the surfaces as clean as possible. I fold and crumple the golden cranes. Inside this small, tidy world, I can maintain order.

N works as a coach and trainer for athletes. I watch a muscle on the back of his arm rise as he shifts around on the couch. So much of the story of his life is visible in his body, a solid mass of strength and damage, a collection of experiences and reactions and corrections. A football lineman, a gymnast, a fighter. When he moves, body parts I didn't used to know about rise and ripple: rear deltoids, latissimus dorsi, trapezius. He is a father, a son, a man, a boy. The parts of him I love most fiercely are the soft ones that balance all his strength: his gentleness, his open heart, his eyes that make and keep contact.

In the apartment we sit with our limbs tangled up, a bowl of berries balanced between us on my knee. I never liked sharing anything until I met him—always preferred my own space, my own bowl, my own chair. Now, I like everything being both of ours. I like sanding down the rough spots of my rigidity, my stubbornness, my ways of being that have ossified over three and a half decades of holding carefully together the boundaries of my heart. Inside our apartment, I feel safe and loved.

Outside, though: disintegration. It is the middle of April and the COVID-19 pandemic is raging. We watch the death rates rising on the news, buy face masks on Amazon, and drop our clothes at the door for decontamination after we go for walks. It's fair to say we are freaked out—me much more than N, who is cooler under the pressures of the unknown. I have spent at least twenty-two hours of each of the last seventy days inside the six hundred square feet of the apartment. I have let many days pass without once stepping outside.

I spend numb hours scrolling through the news, and in every article it sounds like death is imminent, like we are all one bad doorknob touch away from drowning in our own lungs on dry land. My body has just come out of a rough year and feels so vulnerable to infection, infiltration, and compromise that I do not trust its ability to fend off even a regular cold, let alone this new and frightening respiratory virus. My pregnancy feels like a one-time gift, precious and precarious, and protecting it feels more important than anything else I might do. Hence the cranes.

N goes out into the world every day. He goes to work training clients in their private home gyms despite the shelter-in-place order in our state and most of the country. He goes to the grocery store, where he dutifully wears a face mask and fills bags with my favorite treats, the things that make me happy and healthy: greens and root vegetables, sweet potatoes and garlic, different kinds of berries, organic eggs. Dark chocolate and nuts, glistening slabs of grass-fed beef, bubbly waters, slippery oils, crunchy cucumbers. Sweet potato chips and sugar-free coconut milk ice cream. There are more reasons than ever, now, to take care of my body. I have not once been inside a store in the seventy days I have been in quarantine. He has brought and paid for everything I have eaten, waiting in the long lines, navigating the anxious vibrations of the stores, carrying everything up the stairs, cooking me meals from what he has gathered.

Contrary to my fears and expectations, my body is well. It makes me nervous to say so, because the well-being of my body has been so uncertain—since forever, but particularly in the last few years. My body has felt weak and vulnerable, even when it has been growing stronger. But I'll say it anyway: my body is well and strong. Inside this body a small seed of a person is growing, suspended in amniotic fluid. South of my heart: a baby. Our baby.

I wonder if it is better that our baby will never have known a world of high-touch surfaces and carelessly shared meals, if the new normal of masks and distance will not feel like loss to them because they will never have known anything else. On the news I watch as New York—my city, my birthplace, my first home—loses itself, loses everything that makes it what it is and that has made me what I am, and I feel a deep ache that our baby might never know the New York of warm bagels eaten on the subway out of crumpled paper bags, the New York of the Russian baths and La MaMa, halal carts and yellow cabs, hot knishes and greasy Dominican chicken, bodega bacon-egg-and-cheeses but with oat-milk lattes because we stopped drinking bodega coffee a long time ago, paper copies of the *Village Voice*, the fucked-up L train, the smell of schwag weed in the park. Not all those losses are from the virus—not even most of them. Maybe not any of them. It's been a long time coming, this orderly folding in of what once was vivid and ungovernable. I haven't lived back east in nearly ten years. But still, it feels hard, to be so fully of a place that has receded into myth and memory.

Our baby stirs inside me as I drink the one daily cup of black coffee I permit myself. The morning light glints off my pile of half-cranes. I know our baby is safe right now, within me. I have more control now over their well-being than I ever will again, and even though shit is weird, it is also simple.

BRUTALITIES (I)

When I was twenty I got my entire back tattooed, the first pain I paid cash for. Every week, I went to the oldest tattoo shop in Manhattan and sat in a padded leather chair that smelled of iodine. I smashed my face into the upholstery and hunkered down for several hours of paying attention only to what the pain felt like. I did not listen to music or chat with the tattooer or ask for breaks. It took sixty hours over half a year.

Later, when I was thirty, I paid a woman to strap me to a leather cot and hit me with a stick. Stripped of context and ritual, everything in S/M sounds ridiculous. Without any of the euphemistic and oddly formal jargon S/M people are often attached to, the mechanics of the acts sound counterintuitive and depressing. I wanted to get hit with a stick, but I needed it to feel sexual, because I didn't understand any other context for such a desire.

The woman was about my age and made more money than I did. I knew this because I used to do her job.

When I was even younger, still a teenager, I was paid many thousands of dollars to hit men with similar sticks and whips, to punch them in their faces, to kick them between their legs with all the force I could muster. But by thirty I was an adult with a regular job, so I paid the woman three hundred dollars to hit me with the stick for an hour. The more I think about it, the less sense it makes. But it was the only thing that felt clear to me: corporeal tests of how much my body could endure. The sexualizing felt important, but it was just a foil for something deeper and more shameful, of which I had only a fleeting understanding.

In the late nineties, before tattoos and getting hit with sticks had occurred to me, I met Dean. In the back of his metal shop in his building in Bedford-Stuyvesant, he had an old forklift. Its transmission did not work properly and it was largely useless for the task of transporting metal around the shop. He had bought it at the city auction in the Bronx where you could get worn-out generators and school busses with rusted engines, the sort of mechanical refuse no one wanted to deal with, worth more as scrap. The-raise-and lower function of the forks worked fine. He hung a chain fall from the forklift and used it to dangle girls like me, girls who felt lucky to be there, up off the ground with rope.

When I first met Dean, I was so young that I had never yet been with a man who did not live in his childhood home—I had never yet been with a *man*. His building was fantastical, empty of anything practical, full of giant machines that loomed like figures in the corners of the shop. The floor in the loft above the shop was espresso-colored hardwood, the shower head industrial and so powerful I had to kneel under it. He was terribly serious. I didn't see him smile or laugh once until I had known him for weeks, until he had done things to me I didn't yet know the names for.

I adored him almost immediately, but I didn't understand why. It was not a warm love feeling. It was more like hunger. My feelings for him made no sense: we hardly spoke to each other, and I felt incredibly anxious and off-kilter when I was around him. He was so much older than me that we did not share cultural references. Also, he hurt me. My feelings, and my body. He hurt every soft part of me. I left his loft splattered with quickly blackening bruises in the places my clothes covered. Five-finger handprints around my biceps, clicking jawbone, wide bruises and thin red stripes across my ass and thighs. I always dropped everything when he called me. I mopped those espresso-colored floors for him after he fucked me and if he would have asked me for a kidney, I would have found a way to give one to him. He knew this. I was not, it was clear, the first of his acolytes. But I was young and unspoiled, desperately eager to please, and I asked nothing of him, not even to talk. I said yes to everything, so we fit easily, because he was a solid object and I was water and there was nothing I could not shape myself around.

The problem with habitual pain is that you quickly become habituated to it. What at first feels shocking and world-altering becomes routine. When Dean told me to strip and to stand in the corner to wait for the camel whip, I did it. The first time, the hurt of it was so intense that I lost myself. The whip was from Palestine, he told me. It was long and thin and cruel. *A camel must be really big,* I thought when I first saw the whip. I was still half a child, and I thought a child's thoughts. I stood in the corner. Sweat beaded down my ribs and the insides of my thighs. But when it happened, everything changed. One moment I was a person with thoughts and a body and anxieties; I was wondering if I looked ridiculous, standing naked and barefoot facing the wall, I was wondering if my body looked right, if I should have put my hair in a ponytail, if we were going to fuck first or after or at all. I was wondering if I should have been doing something else, thinking something else, if I should have been trying to flirt instead of just obeying like an automaton and then he said *Hold still,* which he didn't have to say because I hadn't moved in fifteen minutes. And then everything was gone except one thing, it was only the hot electric agony stretching from him through the camel whip to the flesh of my ass, there were no words or thoughts, just a high-frequency cracking feeling; something in my core felt caved in and I was falling into where it had collapsed. He was gone and I was too; the feeling was the entire world. I was not *in* pain—I had *become* pain.

I did not move.

He stopped after not too many strikes. Later—years later—he told me he had been afraid, that my refusal to say no had frightened him. That no one had ever not said no before. I took this to mean I was special.

Later, when I was in my twenties, we lived together in a rambling farmhouse in upstate New York, five hours northwest of the city. There were wildflowers growing by the side of the road, large mossy yellow fronds, pink bell shapes bobbling on thin stems, lacy off-white disks that crumpled in the heat. When we first moved to the farm, I cleaned and baked every day. I fed the animals and filled the enamel pitcher with wildflowers, placed it in the center of the sagging wooden table with the carved legs. I imagined that if I acted like the kind of woman who would be treated gently, I would become her, shedding the soiled skin of everything that had already passed between us, stepping into a new life where the air would be warm with sugar and baker's yeast, the touches soft and painless, the tones calm and even. My desire for tenderness was a poorly kept secret, and I understood gentleness, love, and care to be things I had to earn. I was afraid I was undeserving and it frightened me to desire softness, so I bought lots of antique tea towels and I took plates of roasted pork out to him while he was working in his shop, trying to play the role I wanted to be cast in. If I squinted, I could almost see a future: me pregnant, him kind, both of us utterly changed.

At the farm, we had a dog, and the dog developed a problem in his hip. One morning I watched from the loft as Dean pulled him carefully up onto the white linen couch and tucked a down pillow under his haunches. Dean held our dog's face in his big mean hands and stroked the dog's jowls. I couldn't see Dean's face, but I was sure he was crying, those silent tears his sort of men so rarely allow themselves. *Max*, he said to the dog, over and over again. *Max, Max, Max.* I could hear him choking on the tears.

Max, Max, Max. I love you. I love you, I love you. The dog was in pain and we knew it and it broke something open, some new channel that hadn't existed between us before. Taking care of the dog was the kindest thing we ever did together. Dean built the dog an enclosure where he could be outside without hurting himself. He fed him expensive meat and wrapped him in a Pendleton blanket at night. I started to think maybe we could be different, that the man who liked to hit me with his belt had given way to a new man, one whose heart was growing, one who was so broken up over the dog's pain that he could not think of anything else. He was calm, sweet, reasonable. He had feelings just like mine. I stopped baking every day. I forgot about best behavior.

And then it happened again, so fast I lost my breath before his hands even touched my neck. I could always remember the catalytic piece of nonsense, the exact thing that, if I could have swallowed it back down and made it unsaid, would have made everything calm again. This time it was about plastic packing boxes. Sometimes it was about the bumper of a truck, or the mail delivery, or a tone of voice. Once anger sparked, neither of us could control ourselves, we were both picked up by the gale-force swirling of fury between us. My voice became high and accusatory, his eyes went wild, mine streamed tears. He bellowed and I screamed. Once it started, I knew what would eventually happen, and the worst part of me genuinely wanted to see how far it would go, how hard and long he would squeeze his hands around my neck and shake me: until I went black and dizzy and silent? I knew he would not strike me in a furious state. He never did. I knew if he ever hit me out of pure anger I would leave and not come back. At least I thought I knew that. But it was moot, because he didn't, not ever, not once. He hit me only in bed, where the sexualizing rarefied and exonerated the violence, where I could never know if he had saved up all his rage for those moments, or if it was altogether different.

In bed, he always said *Ask for it.*

Please, I always replied.

In anger, he did everything but hit me, which was confusing, because he didn't appear to be in any kind of control.

Soon after we moved to the farm, he started smashing things. An ironstone serving plate, a slow cooker, a Mason jar, a ceramic vase. It did not seem to matter what the object was, only that it was hefty and brittle enough to shatter at my feet or on the wall behind me. He did not ever throw anything directly at me, and this felt important, and it took years for me to understand that the importance of this distinction was sad.

There were phases to the rage, and after he smashed something, if we did not stop fighting, at some point he would draw his body very close to mine and wrap his hands around my familiar neck.

It was different that way. There was, I struggled later to explain to a therapist, nothing in common between this choking and the other kind. There was, I told her, a big difference between choking and hitting. But there was a muscle memory, and the lines of demarcation around my body had been irrevocably blurred by so many years of asking him to cross them.

The upstate farm was where I first felt a shock of recognition at something I saw on a plate. A whole life of eating thighs, breasts, tenderloins, and sweetbreads, served on the bone, black and blue, au jus, and yet I had never fully connected those parts to my own. It was not until I learned to slice into the spare haunches of a spring lamb with a boning knife that I felt an eerie sense of familiarity with the meat. Once it was not neatly parceled out for me by a butcher or a chef, it became parts of a *body*. Loins and sinews and buckled joints, known to me from my own. We didn't talk about it, Dean and I—about the accumulating of animals, the slaughtering, the butchering. We didn't talk about it the same way we didn't talk about his hands around my neck.

Aren't you troubled by all the death around you? a friend in Brooklyn asked me.

Sometimes I wonder if I will die up there, I considered saying, about the farm, but did not. She was silent.

You are so melodramatic, I chided myself.

On a Saturday morning Dean and I killed a pregnant ewe. She had been gestating for so long that the carriage had wasted her body, and all that remained of her apart from her swollen middle were sharp angles under burry chunks of matted wool. To my untrained eye, more than half the weight of her body was in her womb. The ewe was so weak and swollen she could hardly rise from her knees, and the visibility of her cartoonish roundness and alarming bones in such close proximity was grotesque. We had been hoping she would lamb in the night like most of them did— without fuss and without evidence, except the lamb and sometimes a small patch of glistening fluid in the straw. But she didn't lamb and she didn't lamb and she didn't lamb, and every morning when we went out to the barn to check the animals, she was lying on her side, each breath heaving her like she was a great billowing sail. We threw down some grain for her, which was all we knew how to do. She had worms, probably, but we didn't know what to do about it.

Everything at the farm was brutal and undiscussed. We went out to the barn in the morning, me with a bucket and a skinning knife, Dean with the big blade that was just for killing. One of his boots was untied and he had forgotten a belt. His pants sagged as he ambled out past our big turnaround gravel driveway and the stripe of flesh between his pants and jacket was white like a baby's, the only soft part on him. I was drinking coffee out of an under-sized cream-colored cup with a delicate handle and a painting of a bluebell, the sort of cup I associate with softness and femininity, an object of delicacy that wouldn't long survive the lives we were living. In my other hand I held the skinning knife, which was glazed with blood from the last time we did this.

Look at your feet, a shrink with an office that smelled of mold told me. It was an exercise in embodiment, a fix for disassociation. *When you cannot feel your body, look down at your feet, acknowledge where your feet are, and remember that you are where your feet are.* The "you" she was referring to is something skittish and philosophically nebulous. The psyche, the self, I imagine she meant. She did not parse the word. What she did not understand was that the last place I wanted to be was where my feet were.

My feet were standing in a rapidly widening puddle of blood. My cup was on its side, flecked with errant pieces of urine-soaked straw, a small chip missing from its lip. My knife and bucket were in the corner of the milk room, and each of my hands was holding half of the ewe's body cavity, wet and steaming and incredibly resistant to what I was doing, which was spreading it open like I was a heart surgeon, my arms the retractor, straining her open against the laws of anatomy and geometry. Dean sliced into the amniotic sac. I understood that he was trying to save the lamb. The ewe had been dead for two to ten minutes, depending on how you define dead. Blood was still pumping out of the slit he had cut in her neck, but it had slowed to a dribble, flowing down into her sodden wool like ice cream down a child's chin into their shirt. I could see the baby lamb through the filmy sac, not details, just form. It reminded me of the posters outside Planned Parenthood, the ones anti-choice protesters try to crush into patients' lines of vision on their way into the clinic. I could see the lamb's parts. Fluid followed the line of Dean's knife. I was in the way as he reached greedily into the sac, spreading it like the peel of an orange, grabbing for the lamb.

I watched his big meaty hands as they stole the lamb from the messy pile of ewe and sac and fluid and I did not gag. I did not ever feel sick to my stomach. Time had sped up, such that the entire horrific procedure had already occurred in the time it took me to weigh the potential dangers of telling Dean to stop. There was nothing to be saved by stopping him, anyway. I stood there, a mute accomplice, stunned by my silence and my order-following hands. Time had also slowed down, such that I could not yet tell whether the lamb was dead. The motions of its body were slow spasms that may simply have been reactions to all the chaotic movements of the other three bodies around it. Its eyes were sealed shut and its body was covered in so much biological jelly that there was no way to quickly discern the things that indicate life—a suppleness to the skin, pink mucous membranes, a kinetic vibration almost too subtle for the eye to pick up, noticeable only in absence.

When Dean realized the lamb was dead, he placed it on the

smooth concrete floor of the milk room, more gently than I expected. His arms were red-mud brown up past the elbows. Mine were still inside the ewe, I realized with a start. The silence in the milk room was round and swelling, pushing out into all the small cavities, tight to the sashes, rafters, jambs. It rose and filled the room, displacing everything else until Dean stalked out the door without a word. I moved to follow him, but the slam of the door sounded like a personal rebuke, so I sat down in the soiled straw next to the ruined ewe, and I waited.

When the sun was hot and high and the stench of deadness in the milk room became unbearable, I finally left. I cleaned the blood off my hands, my arms, my neck, my clavicle. I threw my clothes in the big industrial trash bin we only remembered to take to the dump when it teemed with maggots. Dean was in the house while I was doing this cleaning, but we did not speak. I went to sleep alone that night, feeling mute and heavy, leaden with the confusion and sadness of the day.

It was impossible for us to speak to each other for days afterward. I tried to think of words to crack the seal on the silence, but I couldn't come up with anything that didn't sound ridiculous, so I said nothing. What had happened on the floor of the milk room was a lurid dramatization of our incompetence, our recklessness, our selfishness. We both knew it, and so we could not speak. This was how we lived with bruised cheekbones, dead fetal animals, broken ocular capillaries. We starved these evidences of oxygen with our prickly silence until they only existed in our discrete imaginations and eventually vaporized, absorbed into the atmosphere of our simmering discomfort.

Dean and I had been doing eyebrow-raising things together for a while, ten years by the time we careened into the tiny hamlet in central New York with his pile of city cash and a truck full of machinery. His rage problem was barely contained and he had been hitting me in my face since the nineties. He was my boy-friend by this point—I wasn't just one of a bunch of girls he hired any longer; he had chosen me, so I did my best to acquiesce to everything he demanded, no matter how painful or humiliating. I had a web of social, sexual, and emotional difficulties I liked to think of as very complicated and exotic, but which reduced to the uncomfortable truth that I was only attracted to men who were mean to me. I felt that I had to hold on to Dean, because he was truly, deeply cruel—diagnosably and gleefully so—but he had another side, too, the side that kept me relatively safe. He had a conscience, or at least a sense of consequence, which is the thing so many men like him lack. His was intermittent; it went into remis-sion for long periods of time and it disappeared in the dark, but it was in him, somewhere. I was never quite afraid of him, though I'm not sure why. Like me, he was smart and self-reflective. He hated the part of himself that was drawn to violence, the part that seemed like it should have belonged to people screaming on daytime talk shows, not to two private-schooled city people who enjoyed bloomy-rind cheeses and Jeff Koons. The part that, for him, had landed him on the wrong end of the worst accusations enough times to constitute a pattern.

Everything I know about Dean's life before me came straight from his mouth. I have my suspicions and instincts, and I've tried to figure out the truth, but the fact is I do not know anything for certain, as I was not there. What he told me was that when he was twenty-two he woke from a blackout in a jail cell in Vermont, in a town not much bigger than the one we lived in, with a head full of questions and blankness where the answers should have been. A woman, his girlfriend, had called 911, saying he had sexually assaulted her. He had been drunk, and jealous, and unhinged. By the time we were at the farm, he hadn't had a drink in twenty years, but back in Vermont he had drunk so hard that he'd had to stop. And even now that he was sober, I knew him and his predilections for slippery slopes well enough to be able to extrapolate what the addition of a blackout might have made him capable of. I had experimented with my ability to say no to him enough times myself to understand that he considered it to be a suggestion. My attempts to say no hadn't stuck—sometimes they hadn't even made it out of my mouth. *She took it back*, he was always careful to mention, about his accuser, and indeed, he walked away from Vermont without any charges. *She brought cookies to the jail the next day. She was my girlfriend. She was drunk too.*

I did not tell anyone about this history. I didn't know exactly what to make of it. It was his, not mine, and it predated me, but I chose him with the full knowledge of this past, those gray-area altercations I often suspected were darker than he liked to think. My feeling is that he did what the woman who called 911 accused him of, so in the context of my own complicity, it didn't matter what had actually happened there: my truth was I believed him capable of sexual assault, and I chose to ignore it.

Then there was the next accusation, this one in the late nineties. What he told me was that this woman was drunk, just like the last one, but this time he had been sober. They were involved in a complicated psychosexual power dynamic, he said, and it had gotten too intense for her. He had harassed her, he told me, had gone to her house in the middle of the night and leaned on the buzzer, and then she had falsely claimed to their mutual friends that he broke into her apartment and punched her in the face, which he vehemently denied. I knew who she was, this second woman. We had many friends in common and I often saw her at gatherings around the city. He told me she was known to be erratic and insane, but he was the only person I'd heard that from. To me, she appeared sweet, and delicate. She spoke in a soft voice and tucked her fluffy blond hair behind her ears a lot. I have no idea what the truth of what happened between them was, but where there's smoke, there's fire, as the saying goes, and some days as I cooked him eggs in our heavy cast-iron griddle I felt as if I was betraying every woman who ever lived.

But I believed people could change. I had changed a lot, myself. How could I not allow him the same possibility? How else could I parse those terrible stories of his violent drunken youth and reconcile them with the man who bottle-fed our first baby goat when the doe wouldn't give the kid her teat? He slept in the barn that night, his body bent into an L shape in the corner of the stall, the doe curled up right next to him, the kid nestled between them. Animals felt safe with him. Children adored him. He took his mother to Paris for her birthday. For years I wore a locket around my neck that he gave to me while singing a John Lennon song, trying to be some guy from a movie, a sweet guy, a romantic guy, the kind of guy you didn't ever have to be afraid of. The kind of guy who would call the veterinarian and make sure the lamb didn't die. The kind of guy who had never stood over a bloody pile of impotent failure in a mess of his own making. A man who doesn't think he is a god.

And so I forgave him, every time. I forgave his character defects and his terrible judgment and most of all I forgave his fatal flaw, that oversize swell of arrogant self-confidence that was both his magic and his ruin. I forgave it because I couldn't think of anything else to do. Three days after the disaster with the lamb, he woke up before me and did all the barn chores. By the time I crawled down the ladder from our loft, he had boiled water for my coffee and left a wire basket full of warm eggs on the kitchen counter. I made the eggs for breakfast, with the slow deliberation I only ever had at our farm, feeling the faintly scalloped texture of the eggshells as I cracked them in my hand, watching the edges of the whites sizzle and crisp up in the shimmering puddle of bacon fat Dean had rendered from our first pig slaughter. We had ramps growing wild at the boggy edge of the property, close to where Dunga Brook babbled when the rain came in hard. Once upon a time the parcel of land we lived on had been a dairy farm, and some mornings when the wind and the moisture were right, I swore I could smell the sweet sour breath of cows in the air around the house.

He came up behind me as I was flipping the eggs. Tiny sparklers of hot fat gnatted at my wrists. He slipped his arms around my belly. He was so much bigger than me that I could feel him all around me, broad arms around my body, scratchy beard on the top of my head. His body was warmer than mine. We hadn't touched each other since we lost the lamb. His body felt like the sun, warming my surface and down into the core of me. I tried to turn around, to look at him, but he held me firmly in place. The whites of the eggs solidified and the membrane over the yolks waxed from shimmering liquid to matte solid. He rested his cheek on the top of my head, and I could hear everything he could not say. *I'm sorry. I wish I could have done better. Thank you. I love you. I'm sorry.* I heard it so loudly and surely that it melted the cold wariness between us.

I would never have ended up at the farm with Dean if I hadn't been good at giving and taking pain. Back when I was a teenager, I worked overnights as a professional dominatrix in Manhattan. I worked for a biker named Cliff, who had rotten teeth hidden under a voluminous beard and always dressed in camouflage fatigues with leather wrist gauntlets, like a character in a B action movie. The biker had picked me up outside the pizza place where I used to go to bum cigarettes when I lived at my parents'. He had told me I was beautiful, pretty enough that I could make a lot of money working for him. That, back then, was all it took.

The biker took 60 percent of my earnings for the dubious service of marketing me. The brand story he used to sell time with me was that I was a particularly sadistic dominatrix: one who really enjoyed administering pain. He arrived at this fiction because I was neither blonde nor Asian and I didn't have big breasts, so I needed a gimmick, something he could condense into one sentence to sell over the phone. This was the nineties, before the internet became what it is today, and most of the men who called had only seen a grainy black-and-white photo of me in one of the oversize paper magazines that listed the dungeons and independent S/M workers in the city. The biker worked the phones, which was off-putting to most of the clients, who expected a solicitous female voice and instead got a gruff Queens accent barking out *Hello, Nutcracker Suite.* So he had to have a good spiel to keep them on the line, and part of that was a marketing niche for each girl. Mine was pain.

The utterly fictive nature of this story must have been evident to the biker. He had a keen predatory nose for the kind of damage that makes girls good sex workers, and he had plucked me off the street even though I had not only zero sex work experience, but hardly even any sex experience. I was good at acting and faking, especially with the clients, but the biker had seen me as a citizen before he turned me into a domme. He had seen me not know what to do with the crops and floggers and lengths of rubber tubing at the dungeon. He'd heard the anxiety in my voice when I'd asked him what I should wear to my first day of work. He even knew my legal name.

So he knew I wasn't the pain queen he sold me as, that I was faking it for tips from the coked-out middle-aged bankers who would come by at three in the morning to be beaten bloody with a rattan cane. He knew my supposed sadistic streak was just a plot twist he had authored, and I knew it too. But the nightly reiterative performance of this newly interesting and lucrative personality twist obscured the truth, and by the time I had quit high school and was beating the bankers full time, six nights a week, the only version of myself I knew was the one he described on the phone. *She's very verbal and intelligent, with a mean streak. She'll hurt you. She's a real sadist.*

At the dungeon, I hurt those men so badly. I was on drugs most of the time, which certainly helped to remove human reactions from the scenes of abjection and agony I was creating, but there was something else, something deeper and more genuine. It wasn't sadism, but something that felt more frightening, a cold spot inside me that could see without feeling.

I watched a thin sweaty man with patches of soft downy gray hair on his chest kneel before me and I beat him until tiny chunks of his flesh whizzed off the surface of his ass. I cut a young lawyer with a razor knife until blood flowed off the table and into the carpet. I kicked a greasy ponytailed man in the testicles over and over again until he collapsed, curled into a ball, and then I pulled his legs out straight and spread them to kick him more. Did I enjoy these performances? I did not. Not in a wet panties kind of way. If they'd given me the same money to just sit and talk, which they sometimes did, I'd have been just as satisfied. But the violence I committed didn't bother me, either. The desperation and the cries of the men didn't touch anything, they just floated over me like a toxic fog headed to another ecosystem. Inside myself, I felt unaltered.

No one had ever hurt *me* like that until Dean walked in. I had never experienced rough touch, despite administering so much of it. The biker didn't let anyone top the girls—not officially, anyway. It was bad for business, he said. In professional S/M circles, the carefully curated image of the sadistic dominatrix is irrevocably altered by the revelation of her taste for pain. Once you've been on your knees, the stain remains. So it was expensive, if you wanted to come into the Nutcracker Suite and beat the girls, and it was also quiet, an off-label backdoor menu offering too sordid to be spoken about even at this place, where getting your face pissed on by a girl in a rubber suit was an utterly unremarkable request.

At the Nutcracker, Dean paid for my time. The biker kept track of what we did there—there were limits, mostly around my subsequent salability. Bruised fruit, that sort of thing. But once Dean started picking me up in front of the armory on Twenty-Second Street, with the pinkish gray dawn light filling his vintage convertible Cadillac and the rising sun holding his profile up with its buoyant brightness as we streaked across the Manhattan Bridge, then there were no limits.

He liked to scare me, but I didn't like that. I didn't like getting tied to his bed frame and threatened with knives and needles. I didn't enjoy feeling afraid. What I enjoyed was how still I could remain while he hurt me. What I liked was endurance: the slow violence of accumulation, time and discomfort building upward and outward and showing me the spaces in myself past where I had thought I ended. I liked seeing how long I could kneel on grains of rice on his hand-hewn floorboards, the skin of my knees dappling in distress, my mouth fixed shut, my voice silent. I liked how terrible it all felt, my face pressed into a musty pile of damp laundry in the corner of his loft, a whip made to spur on a great beast slicing across my small flesh. I liked that I could take it.

Crouched in sweaty anxious fear and splayed out in reckless exhaustion, I found the edges of myself, the only parts I cared to know back then.

When we first came to the farm, I had only hope and a fantasy, roughly drawn with a vague hand, everything pastel-colored and ending with a moral. The longer we stayed, though, the darker that vision turned. The longer we were alone up there, the more lives we took, and the more secrets we accrued, the less I could lie to myself about what was really happening. We were not idealistic artists returning to the land that had borne us. We did not find the authenticity we claimed to be seeking. We were not pursuing a narrow path with love and reverence. This was not

Walden Pond. We were two reckless creatures, fragile and damaged, possessed of too much power in a place we did not understand, trying and failing not to damage each other further. The only true question was how far it would go before something even more terrible happened.

The bloodstain on the milk room floor was wide and dark. I avoided stepping on it when I walked through, but I did not scrub it away, and neither did Dean. We had been chastened by the stunning consequences of our ignorance, and neither of us wanted to forget too quickly that we had made ourselves the gods of this place. When anything on those acres needed help, we were supposed to be responsible. The weight of it staggered me. The terrifying breadth of our power and the consequent vulnerability of the animals was a choking yoke I wanted to run away from.

I wasn't used to holding power—I was more comfortable having it wielded over me. With Dean, I had so little. He was a decade older, nearly a foot taller, and a man, with fancy artist friends and three more zeros in his net worth than I had ever had in my bank account. In our house, there was no illusion of equality. I dreamt of our chickens being eaten by coyotes, our horses tangled in barbed wire, our dog run over by a truck. Sometimes I looked at my feet, like the social worker said to do. They always looked far away, like someone else's parts.

WHAT TO EXPECT WHEN YOU'RE EXPECTING TO POSSIBLY DIE

TUCSON, APRIL 2020, 100°
QUARANTINE WEEK 7, GESTATIONAL WEEK 24

The days and weeks and months of my pregnancy slip by so quickly that I feel pained when I track things like my weight and how much time I have left to pay off my credit card debt. The arrival of the baby is a hard deadline for so many things, the most inelastic one I have ever labored toward, the first one I truly cannot ignore or walk away from. I don't want to, which is lucky.

I read books about childbirth and N joins me in taking a birthing class, which is held on videoconference because of the pandemic. We mute ourselves and eat homemade sweet potato fries and make off-color jokes during the class. *What kind of birth control will you be using after you have your baby?* the facilitator asks. We look at each other and snicker and say *Sixty-nine* at the same time. He takes the last fry off the plate and puts it in my mouth. I worry sometimes that I should be taking the class more seriously, being more intent or intense, but as the time draws nearer—in weeks, because that is how pregnancy time is measured—I feel less and less anxious, more and more sure that I will be fine.

I spent a few tense months in the first trimester of my pregnancy feeling daily mild panic about the not-unlikely chance of my body ripping and tearing. It is not the pain I am afraid of—though I am not unconcerned about that—but the *damage*. I am afraid that after so many years of being a vehicle for hurt, this body that now easily hosts love and pleasure and closeness will be shredded back into a painful thing. I read deep into postpartum internet forums and learned about fourth-degree tears, about prolapses, about bad stitches and incontinence and nicked bladders and diastasis recti. I heard more birth trauma stories than I could hold. Many of my friends who have children were so eager to recount the blood and terror and blades that were part of their children's births that they did not notice my blanching face, my lack of response. I read about dead women, dead babies, bad choices and bad doctors and C. diff. I read too much.

In the sixth month, my belly has swelled enough that being pregnant is the defining feature of my existence. I consider, obsessively, the pros and cons of homebirth. I interview a midwife and talk about little else. I think about bloodstains in our apartment, about amniotic fluid on our bed, about the possibility that I will need more help than an out-of-hospital midwife can offer me. I look at my diminutive bathtub and try to imagine me and N, who hates baths, both crammed into it, the faucet gouging one of our necks, the shower curtain sticking to someone's damp biceps, the floor slippery and the toilet mere inches away. I don't know what to do—I am afraid of the hospital, of COVID, of an institution's ability to seize my bodily autonomy. I think so much that it makes me feel ill, so much that I consider truly unhinged things like wandering into the desert and having my baby in the bed of my truck where no one can touch me or hurt me—or, critically, help me.

We finally decide to use a birthing center—within the hospital, which I hate the thought of, but staffed by midwives rather than doctors, so no grabby male hands on me. As soon as we decide, my fear shifts. I stop looping the body-damage fear thoughts; they are still present but quiet and faded, pixelated in the dusty corners of my mind rather than front and center in high definition.

SICK GAINZ (I)

I n 2016 I was living in Honolulu and I ran so many miles that my heel bone cleaved. I had just started a run when I felt it: a loud, hot twinge in my right foot, as if a piece of cherry-red steel was slicing through me from ankle to sole. When I was honest with myself—and it took several days before I was able to be so—I admitted that I had felt this pain for weeks, perhaps months. Just quieter. Soft enough to ignore.

The dewy mornings always smelled like plumeria and sweet rolls in Pālolo, the valley where I liked to run. On the particular morning when I finally cracked my heel, I'd had a perfect amount of coffee and had gotten enough sleep to power me through the ten miles on my running docket. First, to the back of the valley, behind the Zen center. Back in the lush crevice between the ridges

of the Ko'olau mountain range, crispy mountain apples, like sweet
cucumbers that leave your mouth feeling wet and dry at the same
time, grow by the side of the road, and there's a small store where
you can get sodas and poke bowls.

When the pain announced itself, I immediately turned up the
music in my headphones and took a series of deep breaths, trying
to send the sensation somewhere else. This is a thing I know how
to do: depart my body, be elsewhere. It almost always works. I can
slide a needle into my flesh without flinching. I can look you in
the eye while you punch me in the face. And yet on this particular
day, in the hot sweet wet air, the pain in my foot overtook me, and
I had to stop moving.

On the big screen in my sports medicine doctor's office, the
imaging looked accusatory. The cup of my heel bone, the calca-
neus, was split nearly in half. It had been broken for a while, he
explained to me, tapping on the screen with the butt end of his
pen to indicate the broadening crack between the two pieces of my
bone. I had run more than one hundred miles on a broken heel.

There were good reasons for all this running. Some were
athletic: at five years into my obsessive relationship with long-
distance running, I had found an intensity in my training that
had previously eluded me, and I was on track to run my fastest
marathon by a wide margin. Others were questions of identity that
were soothed by hours of fast-pounding pavement in 85 percent
humidity. The man I was living with had abruptly stopped wanting to have sex with me. I was getting really into my thirties and
it was starting to show in the slope of my ass and the cracks next
to my eyes. I had tabled my ego-inflating career and the bags of

money that came with it for a dubiously charted stab at a creative life. Everything was uncertain, except the mile.

In the mile, I could pour my whole self into pain and exhaustion and let go of all the big questions for a relentless series of the same small question: quit, or keep going? And so I kept going, twenty miles a week, then thirty, forty, through a pain that perhaps I had known wasn't normal. It doesn't matter whether I knew or not, because after two months of hot twinge in my right foot, that day finally came when I lacked the capacity to ignore it for one more second.

You gotta take a rest, my young, sexy, surfer doctor told me, looking me hard in the eye. *No marathon this year.* And there wasn't.

Some facts: when I was young, the only important thing was to be thin. Skinny, skinny, skinny, that's what made you beautiful in the nineties. Thin everything: eyebrows like barely traced pencil lines, thighs like long stretched-out pieces of boneless chicken, arms like little bundles of clothesline, tiny asses disappearing under our tiny skirts, our ribs loud, proud stripes under our gauzy tops. None of these traits was natural to my physique, so I starved myself into many hospitals, into feeding tubes and cans of Ensure, into a fifteen-year collection of eating disorders that finally abated in my late twenties.

I've mostly been well on that front since then. Even as my relationship with exercise twisted into something I was no longer at the helm of, I had been eating good food with great pleasure without considering vomiting it up for many years. I mostly liked how my body looked, and I felt fully comfortable without clothes on, though I always wished for a more feminine shape, sloping breasts and hippy curves to offset my athletic solidity. I considered myself to be in long-term recovery from my eating disorders, as close to normal as someone who had been as sick as I was can get. It had looked for a long time like I was going to be a lifer, of which there are so many—sad, wan forty-somethings carefully counting out pieces of celery. It sucks, it's real, and I remain unspeakably grateful to have been spared the long, drawn-out spiral of that particular variety of suffering.

But wait, my body said. My mind had caught up to a new reality, one in which I was healthy, an athlete, an eater of protein and sweet potatoes, a drinker of water, but inside me there was damage, and not just the stuff I could see or feel. There were things amiss, hormone things, adrenal things, fertility things. My body fat hovered about six percentage points below what it typically takes for a body to menstruate or sustain a pregnancy. And even though I no longer wished to be skinny, I was no less obsessed with my body than I had been a decade earlier. It had just shifted to function over form.

I first learned about physicality and endurance from my father. After the first time I was institutionalized as a teenager, he began running marathons. I hadn't yet run a mile in my life, so I didn't understand the significance of his daily departures in moisture-wicking fabrics and his returns, smelling of salt and radiating either deep self-satisfaction or bitter disappointment. I didn't yet understand that how fast you can travel over ten miles of this earth can determine whether you believe in yourself that day or not. I didn't yet understand that fear and pain and uncertainty can be compressed and moved aside by the cumulative brutality of endurance sport.

A year after my heel fractured, I visited a fertility clinic in Honolulu. I had resumed running with the frantic pent-up energy of a mouse sprung from a trap, and my body felt like a hot engine running without oil. After mentioning that he had taught at Harvard, the doctor looked at my medical history, drew me two graphs and several diagrams, and showed me a PowerPoint presentation on his early-model desktop computer.

When you were in puberty, he told me, pointing at something on the computer that I didn't understand—a gland, maybe? *Your body was starving, and so it didn't . . .*

There is a long blank space there, where I can remember his mouth moving and I can remember a dull crumpling feeling behind my sternum, but I cannot remember what he said.

. . . and that's why you haven't gotten pregnant. You aren't likely to be able to get pregnant without intervention, and definitely not at your current body fat and activity levels.

I felt as though I should cry but I also felt so separated from my body that it would have taken effort to climb back in it and eke tears out. So I didn't cry, and I didn't take notes either, which is why I can't recall any useful information. I just sat there, mute, as he clicked through the rest of the PowerPoint and then I traipsed behind him to the exam room where he smeared cold sticky lubricant on an ultrasound probe and jabbed it inside me, my compliant legs flopping open when he said so, closing back up with a flicker of free-floating shame when he pulled the device out of me with an undignified sucking noise. I paid my bill and I walked around the parking structure for a long time, not really looking for my truck, just walking, wanting to remain in the interstice of what I knew then and what I hadn't known before.

The next thing I remember is lacing my shoes to go for a run.

The honeymoon phase of any addictive behavior is such a swirl of pleasurable brain chemicals and renewed vigor for life that it is, for me, often impossible to turn away from. I've had it with so damn many things I know it by heart, that new-relationship energy of a fresh compulsion. Bourbon, heroin, razor blades, credit cards, dangerous sex, face punching, cash, whiskey, bondage, check fraud, vodka, shoplifting, ketamine, methadone, red wine, cigarettes, work, nicotine gum, croissant binges, wintergreen Skoal. Turning tricks, stealing cash, smoking weed, throwing up, watching porn, eating, starving, trespassing, beating men up. There are so many things that have, for a short while, salved my discomforts and offered me peace and pleasure. I loved those things, once, each and all of them, until they turned on me, like they all did, like they all do. This, of course, is the nature of compulsion. The substance of the habit becomes almost immaterial after so many years of trying to stuff things into the gaping void of spiritual discontent.

But can a spiritual hole be filled with physical acts? And can a body be reasonably expected to endure the battering it might take to reach serenity? The muddled hope that the pains of the body will beget the solace of the mind has been around for as long as people have been keeping track of such things. Yoga, arguably the first recorded form of physical exercise, was developed as a practice to gird body and mind for extended periods of meditation: *these movements will bring you closer to enlightenment.* Victorians used early treadmills as curatives for the wicked instincts of prisoners: *these movements will bring you farther away from the devil.*

There is nothing modern except the details of how I have worn down, burned through, and used up my body. At the end of my CrossFit classes, we all collapse on the ground, heaving, flat on our backs or in the fetal position, leaving behind "sweat angels" in the shapes of our splayed-out bodies when we finally get up.

In 2018, two years after my heel cracked, I moved to Arizona for graduate school and became tired in a new and alarming way. I was lonely and restless in the desert. I wanted to meet people, but I also wanted to be alone. I wanted to date someone, but I was not attracted to anyone I saw or met. Things were looking a bit bleak, and my restlessness started to move from something abstract and emotional to a tangible collection of symptoms: I couldn't sleep very well. I lost my appetite for food. I got confused while driving. So I started running more, braving the one-hundred-plus Arizona heat to get enough miles in to grind down my discomfort. I started lifting weights in a gym in the mornings. I started going to CrossFit.

Soon, my brain soggy with serotonin and norepinephrine from my rapidly increasing workout load, I lacked the time and energy to care that I was lonely. This was the plan. The plan was working. Disassociation is a magical space, like a dream. You cannot stay in it forever, but it has a feeling of timelessness, of being suspended, numb and content. It is a state I imagine resembles, in many ways, true peace, except that it's probably killing you or your life in some tangible way. At night, I gently settled my creaking back onto my memory foam mattress, grateful I didn't have to share the space or the pillows with anyone. In the mornings, I woke up in the air-conditioned dark, grateful I didn't have to tiptoe around anyone's sleep or share the coffee. Soon, I realized I was not lonely anymore. I was happily alone.

I lifted weights twice a day, every day, for three months, and my body changed. Sheets of new muscles appeared in odd places: the sides of my ribs where my bra strap fastened, my shoulder girdle, the creases where my thighs met my hips. The hungry tautness of my running body was supplanted by a new strength, one that made my blazers too small and my sports bras too tight. At my request, my lifting partner, a twenty-two-year-old body builder who lived on sweet potatoes, baked chicken, and pre-workout powder, measured the dimensions of my body. He shook his head seriously when I asked him if he thought I was getting too big.

"Too big?" he repeated, as if he'd never considered those words together, snapping the skin-fold calipers together like castanets. "No! Those are sick gainz!" This, I knew from memes about gym culture, was the highest compliment a millennial gym rat could bestow.

Even as I felt my body consumed by stabs and twinges and crunchy feelings, and a deep and frightening haze of fatigue settled in, I still didn't have words for what I was doing. I wanted to varnish the truth, to obscure it with detail and ritual. But that truth was getting more difficult to justify or ignore or rename when I looked at the spare facts of my existence.

On any given day, I had many things to do aside from exercise.

I was in graduate school, teaching writing to undergrads and free-lancing as a copywriter. Every day, I had pages to write, chapters to read, notes to scribble, lesson plans to compose. Plus, the regular life admin everyone needs to attend to: groceries to buy, hair and truck to wash, batteries to purchase, chicken to cook. I had emails to return, voicemails to answer, a pages-long handwritten letter to read, a missed birthday to make amends for, appointments to schedule. I canceled on my therapist with an hour's notice. I had not managed to find the time to get my eyebrows tended to in over a month. *I am so busy*, I kept hearing myself say, over and over again, in lieu of the apologies I always seemed to half owe to colleagues and loved ones and service providers. I had very nearly blown a freelance deadline that month, the first time I had ever come so close. Where, then, did all the hours go?

In the midst of my body's slow grinding to a halt, I couldn't use adjectives to describe what was wrong with me, only accumulations of facts, piecemeal truths, like these: On an ordinary day, between four thirty in the morning and noon, I would spend more than four hours exercising. I would drive from one gym to another to another, gobbling gummy overboiled slices of sweet potatoes out of a plastic bag in between activities. Later, before the sun went down, I would put on my running shoes and run. Then, I would pull on boxing gloves and hit pads for an hour until my arms were so gelatinous with exhaustion I could barely hold them in front of my face to block my partner's advances.

I performed this series of activities, or similar, on most days. In the limited remaining hours in between training sessions, I was so tired that even simple tasks—returning an email, say, or reading a Best American Essay—often felt overwhelming. I fell asleep reading and regularly lost twenty-minute chunks of time to wandering around trying to remember what I had meant to do next. I hadn't read a full book in months. There was euphoria after each session, so intense at times that I dubbed the feeling "the chemicals" and chased it like I used to chase heroin and cocaine: through exhaustion, through humiliation, through absurdity. But the chemicals didn't last as long as drugs used to, and when they faded I felt stupid and confused, cognitively blunted in a way that perhaps I would have enjoyed if I hadn't had so much to do. My new boyfriend, N, a lifelong athlete and professional coach, told me this dumbed-down feeling was part of what people like about lifting weights. *It makes you a happy dope. That's where the whole "gym bro" thing comes from.*

As all of this was happening, my father and I talked a lot about working out. He was seventy, still athletic but brittle in the way of aging men, a weathered stick at the end of a long winter. For over a year he had been recovering from a broken leg and wasn't able to run more than a couple miles at a time. He was restless: I heard it in his voice when we talked about my mileage, when I told him about the gym. He was skeptical of my new obsession with Cross-Fit and lifting weights. *Careful not to hurt yourself,* he said, *or to get too bulky,* and I understood what he was really cautioning me against was getting too attached to my physical power, that which he was feeling slip through his own fingers.

I didn't want to talk about any of this. I didn't want to talk about it because I was afraid of how anyone I told would look at me, at my soft parts. I didn't want to talk about what I did with my body because then my body would become the unspoken subtopic of every conversation, even those that weren't explicitly about it, and I was afraid that if I then started eating popcorn for dinner and quit going to the gym, I would be seen as failed and lazy in a way that would feel excruciating. I didn't want to be seen like that.

I hadn't had my legs waxed in a while when I went for my appointment with an orthopedic surgeon—*the best hip guy in Arizona*, my physical therapist had told me, looking fangirlish as she enunciated his name. The medical assistant, eyeing my jeans, handed me a pair of disposable shorts cut for a person much larger and taller than me. I changed as requested and my fuzzy legs looked garish in the glaring light of the exam room. When the best hip guy in Arizona finally came into the room, three med students in tow, he took a long look at me from the knees down, clearly diagnosing me as lacking in basic hygiene. Trying to ignore my embarrassment, I relayed my symptoms to him: five years of hip pain, sometimes bad, sometimes not so bad. Sometimes—this part I did not say—so bad it made my breath catch in my throat. There was more that I didn't say, like *Sometimes I stay up late into the night, shifting my weight around my orthopedic mattress, rearranging Lidocaine patches around my body, searching the internet for my symptoms, wondering if it is possible that my iliac crest is fractured.*

He took a brief history and asked what I had done to try to solve the riddle of my pain. Five years of orthopedic specialists, physical therapy, lacrosse balls, stretching, not stretching, strength training, running hills, not running hills, hydrotherapy, massage, acupuncture, dry needling, Bikram yoga, regular yoga, Tiger Balm,

Lidocaine, aspirin, ibuprofen, acetaminophen. He listened to me in a clinical way that was less listening and more waiting for his turn to speak. The medical students were watching him, not me.

The truth of what I wanted in that moment was something outside the scope of what an orthopedic surgeon is trained to provide. It was eleven in the morning, and before my appointment I had lifted weights, practiced yoga for an hour, run seven miles, and gone to a CrossFit class. I was tired, deep-bone tired, a feeling I had trained myself to ignore and to push away with coffee and more physical activity when it demanded my attention. I wanted him to sit down, to look me in both of my eyes, maybe to put his hands on my shoulders in a fatherly way. I wanted him to say, *I see how tired you are. I see how hard you are working. I see there is something broken in your heart. I understand that it feels like if you stop moving, you will die.*

But of course, this is not what he said.

What exercise are you doing currently? he asked me, and by the time I was halfway through my list, he looked up sharply from his computer screen and interrupted me.

Your hip will continue to hurt if you don't scale back your activities, he told me, looking back at the screen and clicking out of a window. *I'm going to send you for an MRI to look for a sacral fracture.*

At this, I startled.

Sacral? Isn't that . . . the back?

Yes, the sacrum, the sacral spine. Often what we see with what presents as hip pain is referred from the spine.

On that particular morning, I had loaded a barbell with one and a quarter times my body weight, rested it on the back of my shoulders, and squatted down to the ground and back ten times in a row, three times. Later, I had jumped on and off a large wooden box more than two hundred times, and then balanced the weight of my body on my head until I toppled over. How many footfalls are there in seven miles? How could my back possibly be broken?

But Doctor, I said, hearing the petulance in my voice, as if I were a small child arguing for more candy and not a thirty-six-year-old woman trying to convince an indifferent doctor that she was not crazy, *How could I be walking around on a broken back and not know it?* I didn't want to talk about any of this because I was afraid if I named it—if I admitted how blurred the line between discipline and compulsion had become—I would jinx it, it would vanish, and all that discipline would dissolve into a cloud of powdered sugar and Marlboro exhale. I would need help lifting large objects onto high shelves and I would cease to be the person who could help older ladies hoist their carry-on luggage into the overhead bin. I was afraid that if I named this thing, I would lose my power. I was afraid that if I named this thing, I would no longer be myself.

Part of the reason my heel—a difficult and unusual bone to break—had split nearly in two is something doctors call the Female Athlete Triad: the interrelationship between inadequate nutrition, loss of the menstrual cycle, and low bone density. You do too much and you don't eat enough and you don't get your period and your bones turn to dust, is the way I understand it.

The Female Athlete Triad disproportionately affects teenage athletes in sports in which body mass or weight is a consideration: gymnasts, dancers, swimmers, runners. Because I had been a teenage hooker and not a teenage athlete, I felt as if I did not quite deserve the title implied by this syndrome. Was I really an *athlete?*

I just exercised a lot. But there were truths I had difficulty deny-
ing, like my oft-missing periods, like my cleaved heel bone, like
the disappearing space between the vertebrae in my lumbar spine,
like my inability to get pregnant.

If I named this thing I might have to relax my promises to
myself, those superstitious announcements of plans that did not,
in any sphere broader than the confines of my own mind, matter. If I said I would run ten miles and I only ran eight, what
was stopping me from sleeping until the afternoon with the curtains drawn and the phone turned off, what was stopping me from
eating an entire loaf of warm brioche with a half a stick of butter until my stomach was shot through with searing pains and
then returning to bed, what was stopping me from not paying
my bills and not taking my vitamins and not returning my messages? What was stopping me from drinking warm bourbon for
breakfast and worming the dulled tips of overused needles into
the soft crooks of my elbows, what was stopping me from any of
the terrible things I could do and have done to myself, back when
my word didn't mean anything?

The name for what was so clearly the matter with me felt like
a lie, and part of why it felt like a lie is that I also occasionally
spent time lazily: writing from a reclining position, indolent like
a fainting Victorian, belly full of berries and sweet potatoes and
pistachio nuts, yet to go out of doors by midmorning and unlikely
to do so for several more hours. *Lazy, lazy, lazy*: I heard this chorus
in my head at most times of the day if I tuned in to that channel,
breaking through the static to catch it like you can catch good
college radio stations in between the dials, hidden between alt-
country and the Jesus station, just peeking through.

You're lazy, you're lazy, you're lazy. Was it my father's voice, he of the midwestern-Germanic work ethic and the negative marathon splits? Or my mother's, a touch shrill from the effort of outpacing generations of immobilizing depression; my mother who claims not to exercise but who rarely stops moving: walk the dog, clean the kitchen, ride the bike, bread store, pork store, vegetable market, chase the kids around at work, chase the dog around the park, shuffle papers around the desk, clean the baseboards, clean the oven, baste the ham, laundry, dusting, driving, biking, walk the dog, clean the windows, dress the salad. She sits for meals and occasionally to make notes in her calendar, but soon she is back up: clean the kitchen, load the dishwasher, fluff the pillows, wash the dog's paws. She doesn't want to work smarter/not harder, because the point isn't the tasks, it is to stay in constant motion. No one has *ever* called my mother lazy.

I didn't want to put a name on what was going on with my life and my body because I wanted to go to the gym, I wanted to go running, I wanted to lift weights, I wanted to go hiking. I wanted to do those activities with friends, I wanted to put pictures of me doing those things on social media, and I wanted everyone who loved me to believe the fiction that I was always having fun, that my pursuits were uncomplicated and joyful, that I was not trying to outpace something large and looming and terrifying. I wanted to keep things cool. I didn't want to talk about the snapping feeling behind my scapula, about the ground-down feeling in my feet, about the flashes of white in my periphery. I didn't want anyone to know how hungry I often was, or how tired I always was, or how much I wished I could be a person who casually ate a doughnut and slept in on Sundays. I didn't want to—but I did. I must have.

I said those things like they were jokes, like they were comedy, like I was doing a bit about an unwell woman for me and my friends to laugh about together. I was afraid admitting any of this would mean I was giving up my seat among the tough. I wanted someone—anyone, really—to see that I was suffering. I wanted someone to see that I had earned a rest. But I was afraid to say so, because what if I sat down and never got back up?

I began lying to the people I loved about how much I was exercising. They were lies of blurring and omission, not commission, at least at first. A lot of rounding-down of hours and avoiding of subjects. *I have an appointment, I'm not available until later, I won't be able to make it tonight.* They were the same well-worn lines of avoidance I had historically used to carve out space to get high, to meet men I shouldn't have been meeting, to avoid eating occasions. They were the bones of the walls I constructed around my secret spaces, and they tumbled out of my mouth without thought, my native tongue.

On the internet, I self-administered a psychometric instrument called the Exercise Addiction Inventory. It was from Dartmouth, so I gave it the benefit of the doubt. I knew from being an addict of so many stripes that taking assessment tests late at night is itself a pretty good indication things have become unmanageable. This test was used by doctors to assess an individual's attitudes toward exercise across six fields, and relied on self-reporting. The statements, which were to be agreed or disagreed with on a scale of 1 to 5, seemed to me ridiculous.

"I use exercise as a way of changing my mood." I thought of the cresting surge of giddiness that sometimes overtook me when I was heaving weights over my head with burned-up lungs, squinting through salty sweat. Why else would you do such a thing, if not to change your mood?

"Conflicts have arisen between me and my family and/or my partner about the amount of exercise I do." This one didn't seem fair. It was so subjective! Could the irritation of my former boyfriend, he of the cigarette habit and the monthly McDonald's run and the cholesterol pills, really be taken as diagnostically significant?

I failed the test somewhat spectacularly, and then administered it to a carefully selected group ("skewed data" is the term, I think) of my friends for comparison, expecting that my fellow CrossFitters or my athlete boyfriend or one of the many former addicts I worked out with would also topple the chart. But they didn't. They rated high-normal, every last one of them, and it was at that point I decided the test was impossibly flawed, authored by couch-people, and was garbage.

I didn't even want to name this thing to myself. Naming is a dangerous game, cousin to truth telling, and I didn't want to tell the truth about this. At four thirty on any morning there was a clanging in my ears. It came from just beside my bed, and also from the kitchen, and also from the bathroom, places around my apartment where I had carefully placed alarm clocks to compel me out of bed hours before I was truly rested. I had been waking up at that hour for long enough that I could usually speed through the most treacherous part of the day: the moment in which it occurred to me, like a flash, that I could just go back to bed. I could lie down, stretch my bare toes deep into the warm pocket of my soft jersey sheets, nestle the side of my face gently into my pile of pillows, enjoy the deep darkness of these secret hours. I could arise refreshed, without purple under my eyes, without nausea in my belly, without the need for several pots of coffee. I could just do it.

I was afraid of this desire, afraid of the sloth that could live within it. I had filed it in the same category as many of my body's other clamorous requests: for the soft mouthfeel of pastry dough, for the burned crackle of a deeply inhaled cigarette, for the warm glow of heroin spreading through the bloodstream, for the depleted peace after violent sex with a stranger. My body, you see, should not be listened to.

And so in the mornings I kept forcing myself to lurch up and stagger from room to room, smashing into door frames with my shoulders, pressing down on the top of each of the alarms. Turn the kettle on. Grind the coffee. Brush my teeth. Count the vitamins out: a handful of earthy-smelling jewels, brown and yellow and burnt sienna, so different from the technicolor Pfizer pills I once started my days with. Fill my coffee mug with ground-up cow's bones, which were supposed to help keep my own bones from breaking.

Now I can say: exercise addiction. *I wish I could have that one instead*, people in twelve-step recovery have said to me, sometimes between drags of cigarettes and bites of stale doughnut. *At least I'd get a good body out of it.* And this is true, if what is meant by "a good body" is visible musculature and a flat stomach.

Sure, I always want to say, *you can have that. But you'll lose things, too.*

You might lose your breasts altogether, the last bastion of softness disappearing into ropey muscle. You might lose your toenails, your friends, your membership at the gym that wouldn't let you lift weights barefoot when you forgot your shoes. You might find yourself urinating in suburban hedges at odd hours of the morning when public bathrooms are not yet open but you are five miles into a run and over hydrated. Your body will become a scattershot of chafe, blister, scab, callous: a constellation of wounding. You will not be as pretty as you once were.

During this time of obsessive strength training, I had 12 percent body fat. I went months without bleeding and imagined my ovaries sitting on their dwindling cache of eggs like judicious hens, giving each other long looks after watching me and my activities, nodding in agreement that they shouldn't spend the precious remaining orbs on my current self, agreeing that they should hold on to them in trust for when I was better equipped to take care. When I did bleed, the blood was often thin and nearly black and always came slowly: a grudging trickle. I'm not a scientist or a doctor, but in the visual language of body fluids, it looked sick, and weak.

YOUR BODY IS A BULL'S EYE

TUCSON, APRIL 2020, 106°
QUARANTINE WEEK 8, GESTATIONAL WEEK 25

The heat I expected in August comes in April, so fast and bright and relentless that I nearly give up on going outside at all. The gyms have closed for the quarantine and I have been going to the small park near our apartment with dumbbells and resistance bands and a large rubber mat, parking myself in the small bit of shade under the large tree on the east side of the park, moving my mat over every twenty minutes or so to chase the movement of the shade patch. I have lugged, in addition to this cumbersome equipment, my increasingly cumbersome body, which no longer easily tolerates things like schlepping eighty pounds of dumbbells in a precariously assembled grasp, which starts to lose breath from just

walking, which grows, seemingly every day, rounder and more conspicuous. I am visibly and undeniably pregnant, and in the park I
discover that instead of the respectful kindness I had expected from
strangers, men on drugs now like to stare at me and masturbate.

The first day I discover this I am doing push-ups in my shade
patch. My friend Maddie—small, delicate in personality and
appearance, nearly invisible in the shadow of a large bush—is sitting across the lawn from me. We are having a periodic shout-
conversation in between the rounds of my workout.

A lean, twitching man jumps out of a parked car and strides
directly toward us with an urgent gait. Growing up in Manhattan embedded me with an extra sense of sorts, one that is always
maintaining awareness of men and danger in the vicinity, one
that usually sifts the harmless from the frightening. I am not, as
a rule, afraid of people who are mentally disturbed or fucked up
on drugs, having spent considerable time in both spaces myself,
so when I do get a feeling of danger, I try to trust it and listen to
it. But I have been gone from New York for a long time, and I've
changed a lot since then. My instincts have dulled, and I've been
on constant high alert to protect my baby from any form of threat
for months now, so I startle more easily, and I question myself.

Yo yo yo, the man mumble-shouts at us. *You pregnant?* I am lifting dumbbells from ground to overhead and am pretty well out
of breath. I am afraid of how close he might come to us. The pandemic and my acute fear of contagion have subtly shifted the balance of power in street interactions: it now feels like everyone is

walking around with a loaded weapon, and all they have to do is breathe. I nod at him and try to make eye contact, but his eyes are wild and roving. *Yes. We really want some space here, can you give us some space?* Now I have dragged my friend into this. He is instantly offended.

Yo, I got a daughter, it's real beautiful, I'm not some creep. He clearly is a creep, but I say *Okay, it's all good, we want space from everyone, because of the virus, it's not just you.* He isn't coming any closer, but he isn't backing away, either. In my mind I can see the molecules of coronavirus spewing out of his nose and mouth, floating through the hot thick air, drifting into my own nose and mouth, traveling through my body and settling into my baby. I understand the way he is looking at me and under any other circumstances I would already have gotten aggressive to try to run him off, but today I am afraid of confrontation, afraid of an unraveling of the situation in which my only recourse would be to literally run away, leaving my truck and my spread of gear and my friend behind.

He wanders away, clearly angry, muttering to himself. I share a long, wide-eyed look with Maddie and pick up my workout where I left off, doing push-ups on my mat. Before I can finish the set, he is back, this time saying things not worth repeating about what he wishes to do to and on my ass. I feel frozen and mute, trapped in the space of the interaction and my fear, furious at my vulnerability and somehow humiliated, though I have done nothing wrong. He is behind me, not too close, but loud, and I let it go on as I finish the set, feeling shame heat up my face and chest. I am wearing tight leggings, my belly is exposed. Somehow, it feels, I have done this. There are people scattered around the park, but no one says or does anything—no one ever does. I am afraid he will come closer and cough or breathe on me. I am equally afraid of how my self-concept will crumble if I hurriedly pack my gear in my bag and scamper off to my truck. I do my last push-up and stand, blood rushing to my face, and turn around to face him.

I hear in my voice the low growly pitch and elevated volume I remember from Brooklyn, from when asserting my space on the street was a daily requirement. *YO.* I am barking, almost. *YOU NEED TO GET THE FUCK AWAY FROM ME.* I start moving toward him, less to close the distance than to let him know I am willing to, that he needs to find his own defensive posture, that I am not an easy target, though I clearly appeared to be one. His body language changes immediately: shoulders down, mouth closed. I feel grateful I have this in me, the ability to puff my chest and assert myself, though truthfully I have very little to back it up. I wonder if men like this know how transparent they are— that we see and understand that they are looking for weakened birds with broken wings and quiet beaks, fearful and mute, easy to prey on. Perhaps I am emboldened by my pregnancy, perhaps by my fear of the virus. Without the broad daylight and other people, I would certainly be less bold. But for now, it works: he turns and shuffles away, and after I watch him gain some distance from us, I resume my workout, flushed with shame and adrenaline but proud of myself for having sent him on his way. I try to talk casually to my friend, but I am more rattled than I want to let on. I turn my head compulsively for the rest of my sets, craning my neck to make sure he hasn't returned.

When I finish my workout, I see him standing far too close to three young hippie chicks who are Hula Hooping on the other side of the park. On another day, I might have gone and helped them, as I wish someone would have helped me. But I choose myself and my baby instead, a conscious betrayal. I take my relief and my shame and my dumbbells and my mat and I say goodbye to my friend and slowly pack my truck, keeping one eye on the man the entire time, and then I drive away, gravel crunching under my tires as he reaches for one of their Hula Hoops.

A VERY BRUTAL GAME

On a Saturday morning, after we drank black coffee out of round-bellied cups, N showed me how to punch him in the face. We were still new, still enjoying lazy hours of just looking at each other, both marveling at what we had found. It was late in the morning and we had slowly disentangled our bodies and climbed out of my bed to stand beneath the high desert sun over my Tucson neighborhood's public park. The heat cut through the crisp dry November air. We nestled the coffee cups at the base of a tree. N showed me how to curl my fingers into a fist that wouldn't break on impact: pinkie finger first, then ring, middle, pointer, each one slightly prouder of the base than the one before, vulnerable thumb curved down behind this protective mass.

"Lead with this knuckle," he told me, tapping on the first joint where my finger met my hand. "And keep your fist in line with your arm, one unbroken line. That's your spear."

As soon as I arrived, Tucson frightened me. I had long been in the habit of going on extended solitary runs in the secret dusk of early mornings and the beckoning cool of sundowns, and as a runner I preferred to do all the things women are instructed not to do: wear headphones, run without a shirt over my sports bra, leave the house without a plan. When I ran, I wanted freedom from the relentless decision tree of contemporary American life. The exercise soothed me into a creature closer to the animal I so often forget I am: mentally calm and physically alert, present in my body rather than my mind.

But the men of Tucson, they were fucking this up. Tucson is a "dark city"—the darkest city of its size in the United States, thanks to a low-light ordinance that strictly limits artificial light to preserve visibility for the many astronomical observatories in Pima County. There are so few lights on many streets that you cannot see a person who is just feet away from you. The men lurched out of bushes, sidled out of recessed doorways, and screeched their trucks over to the shoulders of roads to snarl at me, dangerous like mountain lions, snakes, coyotes. I was used to New York, where everything is brightly lit and desolation is rare. I am not often afraid in New York. But in Tucson, I was afraid of men, and I hated myself for this fear, because I liked to think myself tough. I had cultivated that self-image with years of recklessness that looked like fearlessness. I sought so heedlessly, before, in my younger life, with every strange buzzer I leaned on, every dark building I walked into, every time I said yes to a dodgy proposition.

I was not brave back then. I was numb. It is an important difference. And once I grew up, I was neither. I was well into my thirties when I moved to Tucson, and by then, the preciousness of my life would hit me out of nowhere and I would lose my breath at red lights, in coffee lines, at the gym. It hit me so deep I sometimes cried, fast and sudden, over how much my life mattered to me. I thought, too, about its precarity, and so the wild-eyed, sunparched faces of the bands of men I encountered on the running path by the cavernous dry riverbed and the combination of urban menace and industrial desolation I found on the streets of my new city, they scared me.

When I first met N, who is a Tucson native, a martial artist, and a professional combat coach, I mentioned this fear. He raised an eyebrow.

"Probably not the safest thing, running alone at night."

I was already halfway through my eye roll when he continued.

"But I can teach you how to be safe."

Back in the late nineties and aughts, I wasn't looking for safety from men. Rather, I was actively seeking men who would punch me in the face while we fucked. I wanted intensity, something fierce enough to puncture the suffocating cocoon of numbness I lived inside. Finding those men was more difficult than I imagined. This was the era of AOL chatrooms, the early years of Craigslist. I discovered there were two basic routes, if getting hit is the thing you've decided you need: find a man who knows he likes punching women in the face and hope he doesn't like it *too* much, or find a gentle man and convince him to punch you. Both approaches have drawbacks.

What is wrong with you? was a question I could read into my
friends' long moments of eye contact and the worried furrows
of their foreheads during the years I skulked the nastier corners
of the sex web. They rarely spoke the question out loud, perhaps
because of their familiarity with my proclivities and a vague commitment to sex positivity, but more likely because they knew they
might have found themselves sliced cleanly out of my life for asking such things. Whatever was wrong with me was deeper and
older than any of my friendships. I could have found new friends
more easily than I could have found something else that offered
me the same relief from the bondage of self I got from being
punched in the face.

How does it come to this? my roommate on Greene Avenue once
asked me, gently. It was 2007 by then. I was in my late twenties,
ten years into my deep dive into violent sex. I had just careened
into her dinner party with the white of one eye the color of an
August tomato and the socket around it rapidly turning eggplant
purple. She was weird enough herself that she knew I wouldn't
feel judged by her, exactly. More like inspected.

I can't help what I like, I told her. That turned out not to be true,
but I didn't know so at the time.

In Tucson, the park was studded with clusters of people doing
wholesome brunch-time things. A huge springy gray dog bounded
in circles around his white-bearded person; children climbed the
jungle gym; two couples walked the perimeter, mugs in hands,
their dogs tugging on bright leashes. A leaf blower whined, every
so often accompanied by the lowing hoot of the freight train that
ran through the other side of the neighborhood.

N held the palms of his hands up, just in front and outside of his face. We kicked our slippers off and faced each other, barefoot and squinting. He showed me, with one hand on my shoulder and the other on my hip, how to step, pivot, and throw my fist into his waiting palm. The first time, my body didn't understand. It tried to move the arm independently, my weight planted, my fist carrying little power and glancing flabbily off his hand. By the third time, though, I felt it: the gathering of force rising from foot through legs, hip, trunk, shoulder; the quick shift into a sideways-facing thing shooting all my aliveness into one small place, the shocking *thwack* of my fist on N's hand like sneaker bottoms on pavement, the recoil I felt upon impact traveling back up my arm through to my shoulder. N grinned at me.

"You're good at that."

The first time I was hit in the face, I was a teenager, and I was paid for it. I was seventeen years old, so skinny I could press my knees together without my thighs touching, so doped up on Prozac and mood stabilizers and cocaine it would have taken a rocket launcher to register sensation in my body, which had been so tight with hunger for half its life that I could watch my blood pump through the bluegreen veins that crisscrossed my belly. My habits included staying awake for thirty-six hours at a clip, stubbing cigarettes out on the thin skin of my wrists, and pissing on finance guys' faces for two hundred dollars an hour, money I immediately spent on biscuits and croissants which I vomited into public toilets.

Which is all to say, I was no stranger to the pains of the flesh.

A man with the right scruffed-up beard and breadth of chest swaggered into the S/M dungeon that was my place of business,

and twenty minutes and a handful of cash later had my chin—
still soft with the downy fluff of teengirl skin—held steady in one
paw while the other one flew at my face so hard and fast I ceased
to exist as the same collection of matter I had been just the previous instant. There was a great crack of deafening whiteblankness;
I saw no stars. There were stunned moments of temporary blind-
ness (likely psychosomatic) and a shuffling stagger that gave way
to buckled knees; there was a crumple of girl on shitty fake orien-
tal rug with sweat everywhere and salted metal in the mouth and
a flat clean peace that was the best and quietest moment I'd yet
experienced. Enter Dean.

My job at the dungeon was a consequence of the same numb zeal
that made me say *yes* to everything: any pill or powder, any new
way to touch or be touched. Nothing felt like much of anything,
so I kept looking for whatever was more intense, more extreme.
For the first few weeks that I worked for Cliff, the biker who ran
the dungeon, I crept down the fire stairs of my parents' building
to arrive at work at midnight and lurched back home at seven or
eight in the morning, often sitting in the twenty-four-hour diner
down the block until my parents left the apartment so I wouldn't
have to explain my makeup or my whereabouts.

Once I had made enough money to get my own place, I left
my parents' apartment in the middle of the night with a duffel
bag and no explanation. Leaving home was the culmination of
years of pushing and pulling: my parents never understanding
who I was or what I was running toward, me never feeling like
I could survive my own mind within the confines of our family's life. I was wild, damaged, and reckless. I was hungry for
danger, and I didn't understand why. I didn't fit in my parents'

stable, upper-middle-class world. Once I lived on my own, the dungeon became the whole of my life: not just a job, but a lifestyle. I worked every day and made friends who didn't raise eyebrows at bruises.

I quickly became preoccupied with getting hit. That first open-handed slap from Dean was just the tip of the wedge. Soon, like Camel Lights and pinner joints and powder cocaine, getting slapped was not intense enough. I needed more.

The harder and more brutally I wanted to be hit in the face, the more difficult it was to find a man to do it, at least under the specific conditions I desired: the men had to be hard but never angry. I did not want to feel like I was being battered. I wanted to seek and consent—to feel like what I was serving was a thirst for adventure.

I felt continuously pulled to raise the stakes, to escalate the badness of what I was seeking. I found my way first to the backhand, and later to the closed-fist punch. More harmful and disrespectful than an open-handed slap, the backhand is illegal in boxing and can slice its recipient's face open. Unlike the slap, which can be violent or sensual, or both at once, a backhand is a tool of degradation, carrying heavier cultural implications than an open-handed slap. You can talk a lot of men into some regular slapping and maintain your personhood in their eyes, but once you ask for a backhand—also known as a *pimp slap*—a man has to turn you into something else, a thing rather than a person, to perform it. And to be punched? To be punched is not something you are meant to ask of the kind of men who know your friends or want to hang out with you during the day. It is a violent, complicated request that requires a secretive badness from both parties, but it was what I wanted, and I had been raised by *Cosmopolitan* magazine and *Love Phones* with Dr. Judy to ask for what I desired.

Why did I want this, seek this, demand this? It's a fair question, and it always seems to be the first one. I used to ask it of myself on too-bright mornings in front of mirrors that didn't lie as well as I did. I was asked why by my friends, by my shrinks, by many of the men I asked to hit me. I am asked why today, in my far-saner thirties, when I recount these experiences. But there are holes where the answers should be, a series of absences.

Instead of a neat answer, I want to tell you that the stories you've heard about trauma and violence are reductive. I want to tell you my parents are kind, gentle, loving people, I grew up in peace and safety, I was given education and a voice for my feelings. I was taught I had value. I was taught to respect others and myself. I want to tell you I don't come by violence the way girls come by violence on television and in bad movies. It wasn't given to me. I set out to find it, hungrily but without a clear understanding of what sorts of violence I wanted and what sort I did not.

The real, confounding truth is that I do not have an answer, only observations: in my body, violence has always brought a quickening of the pulse, a fresh tautness to the abdominal muscles, a soft ringing in the ears, the cresting rise of manic euphoria in the chest.

Violence excites me, and I've never experienced a violence more intimate than a punch to the face.

Born into a tradition of combat sport, N has taken more punches to the face than he can recall. In a long, rambling interview, he answered my questions about the violence of his life as a mixed martial artist and coach in a contemplative tone, often pausing for several beats to think before responding. He was driving, so I could watch him closely as he spoke, noting the steadiness of his gaze on the road, the tautness of his broad pectoral muscles as they rose and fell in slow rhythm. He adjusted his neck every few minutes, snapping his chin from side to side and making a sharp crackling sound that I imagined to be the vertebrae of his cervical spine falling into line. His thirty-three-year-old body, altered by years of combat, compact yet visibly powerful, was poised for action even as he sat in the driver's seat.

"Force equals mass times acceleration. A sixteen-ounce sparring glove, though double the mass of an eight-ounce fighting glove, carries less force because the hand inside it cannot accelerate as quickly." I nodded seriously and jotted this information down as N spoke, though the math was somewhat beyond my understanding.

"When you punch someone in the face," he continued, "you don't swing like a bat. You drive like a spear."

As we talked, I realized I was expecting to hear some of the posturing of aggressive, masculinized brutality media has linked, in my mind, to rough sport. I was thinking of Mike Tyson biting off a piece of Evander Holyfield's ear, of Jonathan "War Machine" Koppenhaver nearly murdering his girlfriend in a jealous rage, of Ray Rice dragging his fiancée's battered body out of an elevator. These men: a boxer, a UFC fighter, a football player. Evidence, perhaps, for my suspicion that the violence of sport can serve as a foil for more intimate violence.

But N, a third-generation Hawaiian martial artist, told me that despite the testosterone-soaked marketing of MMA, a true martial artist is playing a sport of self-defense. I, who have never been in a fight and who was never taught to physically defend myself until N did, was rocked by this revelation. When you've never fought, MMA appears so aggressive, so focused on the pursuit and destruction of the opponent. But look closely, and you'll see holes in that assessment, like the way fighters so often check on each other's well-being once the bell has rung to end a round and the way they sometimes hug each other, bloody faces pressing into each other's shoulders, when the fights are over.

"If we're in a fight, I don't really want to hurt you," N explained. "We've just decided to play a very brutal game."

In a fight, a body shot is often less risky and more effective than a blow to the head. So what is it about the face that draws so much of a fighter's attention? To punch someone's face is to invite serious damage to the hand. Yet when we think of brutalities, be they sporting, erotic, or assaultive, a punch to the face is the icon, an act of violence representative of violence itself, laden with semiotics that transcend time, place, and culture.

A fighter who neglects body shots in favor of blows to his opponent's face is called a headhunter. Despite the tactical advantages of going for the liver, the kidneys, the diaphragm, or the floating ribs, N tells me that in a fight, "if we let emotion get in, I'm going to attack your face. That's *you*."

The very flagrancy of this act and the millions of iterations of its performance make it ideal fodder for off-color sex, but in a curious way: a common violence, rendered taboo by repurposing it in a sexual context.

In a cage inside a theater in Phoenix, Arizona, "Cadillac" Le'ville Simpson was bleeding from the nose. I watched, transfixed, as his body deteriorated before my eyes. I had accompanied N to an MMA fight night and he had gone backstage to prepare the fighter he was coaching, leaving me by myself to take in the violence. I was glad to be alone so I could clearly assess the experience I was having. In my body there was a low buzzing where my sternum met my clavicle, a heightened sense of alertness in my limbs.

Simpson had been fighting for just two five-minute rounds, and his face, glazed with the sheen of wet crimson body fluids, had been punched and kicked more times than I was able to count. His face had taken knees, too: *ratatatat*, the staccato slapping of patella on malar and mandible. I scribbled notes furiously in a small notebook.

Trained as an American boxer, Simpson bobbed and weaved his compact body as his opponent, a muay Thai fighter, landed punches with lanky arms that appeared loose until they connected with Simpson's face. From my seat in the third row, twentyish feet away from the action, none of these blows to the head sounded particularly devastating—there was no single sickening crack of bone on bone, which perhaps I expected. There was just the relentless series of quick *thwacks* of Simpson's opponent's fists, sounding like eggs thrown against a wall.

I liked looking at the fighters' bodies. The best of them were rippled with hard, hungry muscles: thick necks and broad chests, limbs visibly capable, even at rest, of inflicting great damage.

The allure of violent men is something I have long struggled to locate the origins of in my personal history. The only truth I can tell about it is that when I was young I felt terribly uncomfortable in my body and my mind and my soul, since always, and violence was one of the few things that muted those discomforts. As a girl, I was what people used to call *troubled* before mental illness became something that is discussed in public: depressed, self-destructive, disordered. I first attempted suicide when I was eleven. I was then sent to a psychiatrist and dutifully swallowed multicolored prescription pills for years without understanding what they were or what they were meant to do. If you told me something would make me feel better, I would try it. I felt that bad. Nothing made me feel better though, and by the time I got to the dungeon and discovered sexualized violence, I was already so well versed in hurting my own body to relieve my mental anguish that bringing someone else into the equation to control and hurt me was, paradoxically, freeing. Under the strong thumb of a rough man, I no longer had to be both actor and acted upon. I could curl up inside myself, all discomforts erased aside from the single and identifiable pain of a blow to the face.

Beyond treating my mental problems with pain, though, I found something undeniably thrilling about getting punched in the face. It is a bad, awful thing to do. The badness of it intoxicates. The flood of neurochemical speedball that rushes in to accompany the mixture of anticipation, fear, desire, and pain felt eerily similar to an armful of cocaine. A punch in the face hurts, but the hurt is generative of other, more interesting sensations; the sensory narrative is one of acute discomfort bursting into euphoria, mania, shock, relief. This is not the way of other hurts, and one needn't be an S/M aficionado to understand this; consider the "funny bone."

I was not, it would seem, alone in my prurient interest in facial violence. In the first episode of the television drama *Californication*, actress Madeline Zima's teenaged character punched David Duchovny's Hank Moody twice in the face while they were having sex. Moody—naked, on his back, approaching orgasm—was clearly not expecting to be punched in the face. He was confused, and perhaps a touch wounded. She did it a second time, and that time he cried out, held his face, and adopted an expression of bemused astonishment as Zima's character kissed him on the cheek, dismounted him, and darted off to the bathroom.

My friend Emma described, with glee, punching a man in the face in bed.

"I was on top, we were going at it . . . He looked up at me and said *Punch me in the face*. And then I cocked my arm back and swung it pretty hard. There was no part of me that wavered."

Imagine, now, if the genders in these scenes were flipped. Imagine, if you will, a man taking giddy and unapologetic delight in clocking a woman in the face. Imagine if she hadn't asked for it or wanted it. Imagine these scenes being laced with a zesty, assertive sexiness rather than brutish violence.

Can you do that? I can't.

There is, in these scenes of sexualized female-on-male violence, an element of script flipping that creates a crack just wide enough for the spectacle to be presented as more punk than disturbing. This is not to say that these violences are inherently sexy or funny. Far from it. Rather, it is to say that in inverting the trope of the rough, dominant man and the vulnerable woman, gender and power receive a remix that is perhaps just subversive enough to be received with fresh eyes. Also, the whole thing is fantasy. We can find the idea of a girl hitting a man funny or twisted rather than somber and devastating because she is punching up, so to speak. She never had any real power to begin with, so when she performs the acts of someone who does, it isn't real, it's roleplay. When men hit women or adults fuck teenagers, they're punching down. It's fresh when Hank Moody gets punched in the face, but it's not funny that he is fucking a teenager. His power is real currency; he doesn't have to grab for it, because it's already in his pocket.

I don't wish to be cavalier about the threads connecting private, desired violence to the myriad ways people harm and exploit each other. I have experienced roughness that existed in the zone between consent and non-consent, and I have asked myself, more than once with genuine confusion, if I was being satisfied or abused. My own receipt of violence came in several overlapping categories: violence I explicitly sought, consented to, and relished; violence I consented to by accepting affection or payment in exchange for it; violence that I did not want, enjoy, or consent to. Getting hit by men I sourced on the internet was different from getting slapped in the face in the dungeon was different from Dean's rageful choking. The connection between these three different sets of scenes was me—my body, my choices, the physical actions I received. But the experiences could not have been more different in tenor and tone. Because I have felt, with my own body, each of these experiences of violence, I understand a few things that can only be reported live from the scene: violences are as different from each other as kisses are. One variety of violence does not necessarily inform another. As with all sexual acts, an act of violence is only a signifier, and what is signified is determined by context and dynamic.

Still, it is difficult to untangle violence from subjugation and trauma. The attempt to do so is a dicey enterprise, culturally speaking. For many people who are harmed at the hands of others who abuse power and violence, it is safer and better, and at times necessary, to dismiss roughness altogether. If we say gentle touch is the only ethical touch, that is a clear and easy boundary to abide by. But that boundary also elides the lived experience of a lot of people, including myself, who are drawn to roughness in its various forms and who seek outlets for those urges.

When I was young there was a constant element of danger, psychological and otherwise, embedded in my preoccupation with violence and extremity. As an older and saner person, I no longer have any interest in that danger, or in damage. I remain, however, drawn in by the pull of violence. That pull was what I had first felt watching the fights, a magnetic feeling I had no explanation for, only abstract feelings more sensory than emotional.

Essayist Kerry Howley describes watching her first MMA fight like so: "I was very excited by the spectacle . . . I had for the first time in my life, found a way out of this, my own skin. My experience echoed precisely descriptions handed down in the writings of Schopenhauer, Nietzsche, and Artaud, in which a disturbing ritual—often violent—rendered each of their senses many times more acute, as if the dull blunt body were momentarily transformed into a tuning fork, alive, as Schopenhauer put it, 'to sensations fine and fleeting.' Some have called the feeling *ecstasy*."

I am as perplexed as anyone by my relationship with violence, and by the question of how to integrate it into the rest of my life, politics, and identity. I know that when I am transformed into the tuning fork, I am able to both occupy and depart myself in a way that is more compelling than perhaps any other human experience I know.

What does this mean about me—about who I am, and about how fucked up I am? I am not sure. Where, I keep wondering, might I house my persistent interest in violence on the grid of what is acceptable and what is—to deploy a term that is increasingly used to describe the bulk of my curiosities and desires—problematic? What does it mean that now, deep into my thirties with a partner who is at once powerful and gentle, I am no longer interested in getting hit but I am still circling violence, ever finding new ways back to it?

"Human sexuality is a complicated phenomenon," Patrick Califia reminded us back in 1994 in *Public Sex: The Culture of Radical Sex*. "A cursory examination will not yield the entire significance of a sexual act." When I think about the fights in the cage, about *Californication*, about my friend Emma's anecdote, and about my own fixation with getting hit, I am comforted by this reminder. It suggests to me that the meanings to be made by examining proclivities—yours, mine, anyone's—are too idiosyncratic to conform to valuation and categorization, and that they are as prone as anything to shifting and changing over time.

The call to violence summons people along some well-trodden paths, some more socially acceptable than others. Sport provides a cover of sorts for those who wish to witness and commit bodily brutalities, and there is no modern sport more violent than mixed martial arts.

For many practitioners of traditional martial arts like judo, karate, and muay Thai, there is a desire to distance their practices from testosterone-fueled American MMA, with its gladiatorial rhetoric of unhinged aggression. Jujitsu, in particular, is an art of self-defense, developed not for the pageantry of athletic competition, but for protection of self and family during times of strife and violence.

And yet. Men are fighting each other to the point of unconsciousness, in steel cages, in theaters and arenas, for the spectacular pleasure of crowds who scream things like *Break his arm*, *Fuck him up*, *Kill him*, and "Uh vai morrer," which means *You're gonna die* in Brazilian Portuguese. In twenty-first-century America, in Phoenix, in Las Vegas, in Atlantic City, modernity and social progress fall away as crowds scream themselves hoarse at warring bodies as they clash and rend and break, the mats in the cages soiled with the timeless stains of sweat and blood.

There is an idea that there is freedom in plumbing the depths of the psyche and locating the origins of troublesome behavior. In service to this idea, I have spent many thousands of dollars and hours on therapy, sat in the uncomfortable chairs of twelve-step programs, and read the books of countless self-help gurus with equal parts hope and resignation. In this seeking, I found few answers, none specific enough to quell my curiosity or solve my problems. Along the way I lost the conviction that uncovering the whys of my ways was a worthwhile enterprise. I did not grow up in violence, did not witness it as a child, did not have a relationship to it until I sought it in my sexual life. It didn't make sense that a girl who was offered all the support and cultivation my family tried to give me would have ended up where I did. Yet I flowed so thoughtlessly into sex violence that it seemed there must have been some programming at work, a predestination that could explain my inexplicable wants.

It was not until time passed and my desires shifted that I could see any of this with clarity. I never tried to quit wanting to be hurt. It seemed like a deep and unshakeable truth, and also a great source of relief from what I understood to be my unrelated *real problems*. But as with many compulsions that drive us and save us and then ruin our lives, the habit must be stopped before any true change can occur. Once I was touched gently and truly enjoyed it, I could no longer see wanting to get punched as adventurous. I can only see it, now, for myself, as the panicked squirming of a creature too restless to properly exist in its own body.

I can't help what I like was something I said a lot in my twenties. When I was young and bruised and my face only felt beautiful under the cover of thick, concealing makeup, I thought I was powerless over my desires. I thought sexuality—mine, at least—was both fixed and inevitable, coded in me like hazel eyes and brown hair. In that conception of identity, preferences take the form of unalterable truths: I enjoy salty foods. I detest being cold. The only men I am attracted to are those with relationships to violence.

What I didn't look hard enough to see, though, are these additional truths: I once stopped eating salt for a month and after that experiment a small pinch of Maldon tasted unbearable. Years ago, I spent three straight winters working outdoors in New York City, and after those seasons I no longer shivered when the temperature dropped below sixty. What I am saying is maybe what feels pre-ordained might in fact be the result of a series of actions and reactions at once too vast and too minute to identify. I was transfixed by violence and power, and maybe I still am, and maybe I always will be, and maybe I will never fully understand why. But my relationship to violence and my desire to be hurt have been altered over time, and today I no longer need or wish to be the object upon which violence is exerted.

I feel sad sometimes when I think about how young and small and desperate I was back when I was getting hit a lot. I didn't understand that my compulsion for extremity was really just an inversion of my restlessness and discontentment. I mistook being *out there* for having a personality. When I got more comfortable in my life, my self, my body, I began to want different things. Pleasure over pain. Peace over chaos. It was a slow shift, marked by encounters I was startled to find unpleasant, ones which I once would have enjoyed.

In the five years that passed between the last time I saw Dean and the first time I saw N, the men I chose to be with each felt slightly off, as if there was a glitch between the part of me that was drawn to them and the part of me that actually experienced them. Sometimes I asked for violence and did not fully enjoy it when I received it. Sometimes I locked eyes with men whose hands would later feel wrong, whose bodies would feel off. Sometimes I asked for roughness from men who did not want to be rough and then I became frustrated that they weren't better at it. Sometimes I tried to find connection with men who appeared present but felt vacant. I hovered, always, in a space between presence and vacancy myself.

The last man I slept with before N was someone my twenty-year-old self would have become obsessed with. He would meet me at the back of my truck, in the belly of his boat, and behind rockpiles on the sides of the highway. He was aggressive but not crazy, an ultimately decent person who also knew how to press on my neck to make me black out in thirty seconds and was glad to do so. But he never felt quite right, and though I enjoyed him, I always wanted to leave, alone, when we were done.

At the end of each of these misalignments, I became convinced I was done with sex, that there was no touch that would feel good and correct, no body whose presence would feel better than being alone. I did not understand that I had changed, that I was ready for something different, something I hadn't yet been still or brave enough for.

When I first met N I wondered, in the way we always wonder about people we are attracted to, how he would feel. How he would touch me, speak to me, move me. What he would want, who he would be, when we slept together. I hung around his gym and watched him punch and kick and elbow and knee people. I saw the power of his body and I wondered about the containment system for that violence, how it would find its way into his touch, how I would match it.

We spent a lot of time together at his gym, him teaching me body movements meant to heal my chronic athletic pain, before we were ever alone together. On an early day, when I still barely knew him, he placed his hand on the back of my neck to show me how to articulate my cervical spine, and I knew as soon as I felt his touch that he would never hurt me, not if I asked, not under any

circumstances. There was a gentleness in his fingers, an awareness of exactly what he was doing and exactly what it was doing to
me, that I had never felt from anyone before.

In Tucson, in another park on another Saturday, N showed me how
to kick him in the liver. He placed my outstretched foot against
the most exposed part of his torso, showing me exactly where to
make contact, in the soft part between ribs and pelvis. *Step, pivot,
kick.* He showed me which part of my leg to strike with: the lowest
part of the tibia, directly above the ankle. I struggled to balance
on one leg. There was a catch in my hip, a twinge in my ankle, a
disconnect between my upper and lower bodies. I couldn't imagine using the action to defend myself. N told me I was doing great
and I mostly didn't believe him, but a tiny part of me felt strong
and tough and resilient. After thirty or so kicks, my legs didn't feel
quite so incapable.

"Want to play a pain game?" he asked me, and for an instant I
was in the dungeon again, not yet programmed with the words *No
thank you*, ever tilting my face upward to request the attentions of
an unkind hand. Dean used to ask me questions like this.

The difference between a man who loves me and a man who
merely loves that I can take pain was clear, so clear that it was difficult to retrace the steps back to the time when they were conflated.

The instant passed and I saw N's face in front of me: smile wide,
eyes kind. He was, of course, joking. The pain game: more leg
exercises, in which we took turns kicking each other's femurs with
just slightly less restraint than before. He shifted his weight from

foot to foot and held his hands up in the Thai boxing stance. In the fluid movements of his body I saw lion, panther, tiger, fighter. He could kill me, or probably anyone, with his hands.

I kicked him in the thigh, and though my movement lacked grace, I did connect, and his face broke into a grin.

"Nice."

His turn, then. He pivoted on one foot, faster than I could track with my eyes, and kicked me as gently as a big dog cuffing a puppy. It smarted—the tibia is harder and sharper than I knew, and the femur richer with nerve endings—but it was a small pain, measured and localized, and it taught me something useful about the truths of the body.

Later, I made us breakfast salads. My apartment was flooded with the downy white light of late morning, and I watched N as he ate, his face guileless. The small pleasures of the morning—my clean hair falling like a curtain on my bare back, the bright crunch of sliced fennel, the rough weave of the blanket under my thighs— felt utterly satisfying.

N told me about body tempering: the process by which the tissues of a body become acclimated to accepting force. A fighter's body is able to receive blows that would kill a regular person. The fighter can receive many of them, one after the other, and remain standing, because the cells of their body have been altered. The fighter's body has been trained, through force, to receive violence.

I wondered about the inverse effect, about what is communicated by the absence of force. Do cells understand gentleness, too? In Tucson, my face had been touched only by N's careful hands, and I could not help but wonder if my newfound ability to take pleasure in the grace of the everyday was related.

A few years had passed since I was last punched in the face. I appeared softer than I once did. When I look at photographs of myself taken in my twenties, there was a fixedness to my jaw that has since vanished, a scowl that has lifted. The teeth that once crumbled have been repaired. I finally let go of my dogged pursuit of more, faster, harder, worse.

I regret none of the seeking I did. Not one strike, not one moment. I know in a deep true place that I needed all those blows to the face, all those not-quite-right moments, to finally understand the tremendous power of gentle love.

THE FAST SLOWDOWN

As spring stretches toward summer and I grow more and more pregnant, new discomforts appear in my body: deep aching throbs in the creases of my hips, hot acid churning in my stomach, tenderness in the large erector muscles of my lower back. They are human pains—normal human pains. Small and contained and knowable, pains that can be described and ignored, pains that can be taken to bed. My body is free, for now at least, of the kinds of pains I used to inflict on myself: hot and searing, fundamentally violent even when they were slow and silent, chaotic in sensation and difficult to distill into words.

I used to hurt myself so much in private that my relationship with myself became a cave of pain, interchanging mental anguish with the harsh stabs of neglect, abuse, and deterioration. Not until my body became a vessel to care for another human did I begin to understand the depths of how terribly I have cared for it, and for myself.

When I was training for marathons I thought of running first thing upon awakening. How many miles? Which route? Would I eat? If so, what and when? Would I allow myself any breaks? I thought, too, of running when I creaked into bed at night with a round swelling of self-satisfaction if I went far enough and fast enough, the sour clang of self-loathing if I did not. And if I skipped my run altogether? For that I would earn a degree of hate for myself I have never experienced for another person, feeling undeserving of my existence and choked by a deep fast gloom that occupied all of the horizon.

I don't run anymore, not now at least. N and I ran some when we first met, quick shirtless miles looping around the streets of our neighborhood and the dusty snaking trails in the hills west of town. I loved running with him—it is not his sport and never really was, but he did it with me, often better than me, his bare sunbrowned back ahead of me on the trail blocking the glare from my eyes, his strong legs moving with patience and efficiency, his stride steady and free of the erratic accelerations and decelerations that mark mine, his footfalls sounding like unshod horses. We would hug, sweaty, as soon as we stopped, our bodies hot and slick and sometimes heaving. We tried to enter the New York City marathon together, even though he's never run farther than seven miles and I was once firmly convinced I would never want to run a marathon with another person. It felt like an intrusion of the best kind, our running together, taking a thing I had initially thought was about liberation, but that turned out to also really be about self-abuse, and bringing it into the light, a thing to share. Running didn't *mean* so much with him—it didn't mean I was or was not valid as a person, or that my body was or wasn't acceptable or that I did or did not deserve food and sleep and rest. Running was just moving our bodies.

It started to feel heavy and awkward to run about halfway through my pregnancy, but I kept trying for a while. One afternoon early into quarantine, hiking on a trail east of town where we went to escape the confinement of the apartment, I felt so moved by the air on my skin and the beckoning path in front of us that I looked at N and asked *Do you want to?* He looked at me and said *Sure*, and I pulled my shirt off, wrapped it around my wrist, and broke into a trot. It was briefly thrilling to be moving faster than a walk. My legs felt strong. Nothing hurt. But after just a few minutes I was so out of breath that I had to stop. It felt like my lungs were trying to expand but were being held in a vise. Pulling the thick elastic band of my sports bra away from my sternum, I sucked in air and gestured wildly at N. *Can you cut this? I can't breathe.* He steadied me at the edge of the trail, took his knife out, and pulled the band away from my back. *Are you sure? It's going to be ruined.* I didn't care. As soon as he sliced through the band, leaving me with just the looser top fabric intact, I felt normal, my lungs, unfettered. We ran the rest of the trail, me gulping big heaving mouthfuls of air with the thirst of the dehydrated, my feet moving faster than they had in months, dusty pebbles spraying from the soles of our shoes.

When we got home, I pulled the bra off and took a good look at it. I didn't understand why it had gotten so tight—my breasts had grown a lot, yes, but the band that was compressing me into hyperventilation fit below them, over my ribcage. I went to the mirror in the bathroom, to inspect myself and see if somehow my ribs had become covered in a new layer of flesh, but no, there they were, protruding visibly as they always have. On a hunch I pulled out a soft tape measure and measured their circumference. This is a measurement anyone who wears a bra knows offhand—it's the "34" in "34C." Mine had always been 30 inches until I started weightlifting and my lats got strong—since then, 32 inches. The tape measure read 35. I smoothed it out and checked again, certain it had been twisted, but again it read 35. I felt all along my ribcage, probing for pockets of excess skin or fat, but there were none. If anything, the skin felt spread very thin, the way chicken skin stretches over the knobby bones of the wings.

On the internet, I learned that my ribs had expanded—that they had done so to make room for my organs, which were being squashed up into the crawl spaces of my abdomen to make room for my growing uterus, placenta, and baby. I learned, too, that my uterus was likely pressing on my diaphragm, making it impossible to get a full deep breath. Hence the gulping, the thirsty-for-air feeling. I found this information oddly stunning—that I could grow and spread so much without feeling it happen, that only a garment clued me in to these measurable changes in my body.

Now that I am in my sixth month of pregnancy, it feels distinctly shitty to run. I lose my breath almost immediately and struggle to regain it even at a very slow pace. I think it is not great for my baby for me to be so out of breath, so I take breaks, which feels oddly fine. This is a body I can listen to, now. This is a body that can speak its needs. After even a short jog I feel a prickly cramping weight in my abdomen and pelvic floor for hours, as if my bladder has been punched and pummeled, which in some ways it has been. I watch, on the internet, equally pregnant women working out much harder than I am working out and I feel mild anxiety that I am letting my fitness go, that I am getting weak, that I need to push harder, but the thought passes every time.

I ask N if I am being lazy, if I'm losing my grip on my strength and conditioning. I trust him as my coach not to lie to me. I trust him. He tells me that I am fine, that I am fit, that it is okay to hear my body and be easy sometimes and that fitness doesn't vanish as if it never existed, not this fast anyway. He tells me, though not in these exact words, that my body is good enough and strong enough and I am working hard enough. He tells me, though not in these exact words, that I am enough.

Once a week I drive twelve miles north to the twenty acres of desert land where N's mom lives. I swim in the pool with N and his three-year-old son, trying to stay close to this little boy despite the complicated logistics of a rapidly blending family in a pandemic quarantine. N's mom makes us brunch and it is in many ways the highlight of my week, the only moment of family or community that exists outside of the internet during my quarantine. His mom is wonderful—warm and kind and honest—and I understand, when I am with her, some of how he came to be so good.

On my drive up I pass the same woman every time, running. It is usually about ten in the morning, the sun hot and high and only getting hotter and higher, the temperature edging close to one hundred degrees, the UV searing. This is death heat, hell heat, punishment. Everyone sane is indoors or by a pool. But this woman, she runs, her spindly limbs pushing through the blanket of heat, her visored face smeared with white zinc. I know her. I see her. I have been her. I suspect that she has a comfortable home she could be sitting in, that she is out here for bad reasons, hateful reasons, that she does not feel like enough until and unless she pounds out these hot awful miles, that they are the only things that make her feel alive and also that they are absolutely wrecking her body, that she creaks and aches and crunches, that she sits in the bath so long the water goes cold trying to eke as many moments of relief as she can out of the tub. I feel, every time I pass her, deep gratitude that I do not have to do that today, that I can sit by the pool and eat eggs and avocado and feel my baby wriggle around and hate myself in a small enough proportion that I can hold it in my hand, crumple it like paper, and toss it aside to be dealt with another day.

WORKING

Sex Work Is Real Work

In Tucson, which thinks of itself as progressive but is no New York City, I went to see the movie *Hustlers* wearing a shirt that read SOMEONE YOU LOVE IS A SEX WORKER. In the theater lobby, I received a few sneery looks. I watched the movie, a ripped-from-the-headlines blockbuster indie about a group of enterprising strippers who wanted to level up their hustle by any means necessary, with a small group of my friends from graduate school—people who have not worked the way I used to work.

After the movie, we were all chatting in the parking lot and I said *worked* to them and realized it didn't mean to them what it does to me. To them, *working* just meant labor for money: a job. That's work, too, but when I say *working*, as in, *when I was working*, it means a specific thing that girls who have also *worked* don't ever misunderstand. To be working like I meant it is not just to perform labor for money. It is, no matter what kind of sex work you do, to become a wholly different person for however long, to take your own human reactions, thoughts, and desires and hide them so completely that they are not even on the table for consideration. It doesn't matter how fucked up your life is in any moment, or how great: to work, you put it away. The same can be said of any job that requires emotional labor—ask any good waitress or nurse. I pasted the same smile on my face for cocktail waitressing that I did for dominatrixing, and sex work taught me many of the interpersonal skills that serve me well as an academic. Sex work is work, but the way sex work is understood and policed in our carceral state makes it an unshakeable identity as well. If you hold Schrödinger's job title, you are at once a worker and a whore.

Everyone in our little group was stoked for the hustle depicted in the movie. The theater rang with hoots of delight when the women on the screen secured their bags. Somewhere between *Showgirls* and Cardi B, sex work had received an image overhaul. At least on the internet, the line between Regular Girl and Hooker had become blurrier. Earlier that same year, Hollywood actress Bella Thorne had made a cool million on her first day as talent on the erotic content platform OnlyFans. "Porn star" had become "content creator," and a legion of eighteen-year-old girls had been groomed to misunderstand online sex work as a fast and easy way to make a ton of money without ever having to touch or be touched.

My experience predates this rebranding. When I was working, no one outside of the industry thought sex work was particularly cool or sexy or chic. I worked for ten years. I started when I was a teenager. The first dollar I ever made was as a sex worker. It was a job—an identity, too, to be sure, but also simply the way I paid my rent. The truth of those years is that I worked when I was sick, I worked when I was well, I worked when I was an addict, and I worked when I got sober. I chose to work. I needed the money, yes, but not any more than anyone else. My mom got sick, and I worked. My boyfriends and I fought, and I worked. One of the girls I worked with had knee surgery and she worked for months in a walking cast. To have a place to go where you put on a face designed to make your client feel a certain way is a refuge, and also a jail.

During the beginning of the movie there were scenes full of cash and good shoes and car service black cars. That was true for me sometimes, but there were also the bad vinyl stripper shoes we all wore—Pleasers—and the subway and paying for cigarettes with change. I made a lot of money working, but I wasn't ever able to hang on to it.

For a long time after I retired, going back was a regular reflexive thought. For one session, one night, one week, one year. A contained amount of time, not a lifestyle like before. Once I became too old to work the way I'd want to—with the kind of power that only comes from beauty and either youth or excellent plastic surgery—I thought about it less, but still. Sometimes.

It baffles me, looking back, how little attention I paid to the care of my body when I was working, while paying incredible attention to its surfaces. I had a gym membership and, briefly, a trainer, but I smoked two packs of cigarettes a day and for much of my working life I drank so much alcohol that even though I was skinny, I was also always puffy. My body was the instrument of my work, but it felt so unrelated to me that I treated it more like a possession than anything else. I spent a great deal of money on hair removal and latex clothing and manicures. I spent a great deal of money on taxis. I spent a great deal of money on my boyfriend, a jobless wonder who was great on a bass guitar and not good for much else.

As a professional dominatrix, I went by my real first name, which is something of a cardinal sin in sex work. I didn't know any better when I started, and by the time I realized, it seemed too late to change. I made up a fake alliterative last name that sounded porny in a way I liked, and Margo M. became my working name, which quickly started to feel like my real name. From the very beginning, there was a blurring of myself and my persona as a sex worker (which is a good example of why it's best to wait until you have one fully formed personality before taking on a second). Unlike a lot of the women I worked with, my working persona wasn't a foil to my preexisting self. Rather, I kept their overlap as complete as I was able. Switching back and forth made me feel like a fraud on both sides.

I ate nearly all my meals from restaurant takeout. I had a pink flip phone that was only for business calls, which I took in the basement apartment I shared with the bass player and our three dogs. I wore lipstick constantly. My skirts were so short my butt cheeks peeked out when I crossed my legs. My mother doesn't wear makeup or heels or any other high-femme accoutrements, so I learned how to draw a lip line, straighten a Cuban heel, and carry my cash in my bra from the girls I worked with. I learned other things from them, too: how to stay up all night without sleeping (cocaine), how to make enemies (steal clients), how to avoid arrest (no one really knew, but we were lucky and called it smart). I wore a lot of leather and latex and garter belts. I washed my pussy in the sink.

For a while, I thought working was the best thing that could happen to a person. Like I'd been chosen or something. I watched the civilian girls I knew wake up early, put on their makeup on the train, drink coffee out of paper cups they'd leave nude-mauve lipstick stains on, be tired. I saw bartenders, receptionists, real-job girls, retail chicks, baby lawyers moving through the city, tired and late, and I felt sorry for all of them. Me, I was tired all the time too, but from partying and working nights. And I was late, too—hours late, days late sometimes—but I hadn't yet learned to feel anxiety about it, so I just showed up when I showed up.

My clients sent me black Lincoln Town Cars. My clients gave me credit cards with my working name on them. My clients took me to dinners where I would pick at my food and then bring home the leftovers for the bass player. My clients brought me expensive gifts I never really wanted.

I worried about money a lot when I was working. It was always coming in, but unpredictably, droughts and monsoons only. It was always going out, too, that pace much more reliable, manicure dinner taxi shoes, drinks brunch dress makeup. I paid the tab every single time the bass player and I went anywhere, and when I hung out with girls who weren't working, I paid the tab for them too. I bought vacations and bicycles and guitars, amplifiers and dog surgeries and shrink appointments. I paid for everything in cash.

Since retiring from sex work, I've had two careers, and I've made money, but never the bloated influxes of cash I got used to in my late teens and early twenties. As a writer, I will never make anything close to my lawyer father's salary, and I will never be able to give my child the same financial ease he gave to me and my siblings. In 2019, when *Hustlers* came out, it was nearly fifteen years after I had made my last sex work dollar. I was living on a graduate school stipend and at the beginning of each month I would take three hundred dollars in cash out of the bank and try to stretch it for a whole month, for coffees and salads and things like that, the daily costs of being a human in a city. Back when I had lived in upstate New York on a farm, I spent zero dollars a month after I put gas in my truck, but that was a different life, with costs of its own, like all of them.

Despite understanding the nuances of all this quality-of-life math, I never lost the urge to buy my friends taxi rides and coffees and small objects—things that make life feel sweet and easy for a moment. I missed, most of all, taking my friends out to absurdly priced meals and paying. I missed a client's signature on the AmEx bill. But money never made me feel safe, just sparkly.

Manhattan

Two years before the Twin Towers came down, I first came into something that felt like power. It started on the streets in Manhattan, right around when I turned seventeen and became, in the same year, way hotter and marginally less stupid than I'd been at sixteen. I remember feeling the altered gaze of men, feeling how they no longer stared as long as they wanted to, articulating their necks from collarbone to sky. Now, they looked more carefully, letting their eyes flit away when I looked back, feeling the shame of having encroached on something out of their price range.

Men have always looked at me. Part of this is just that I grew up in New York: a pedestrian shopping mall of girls, milling about in a gaze economy. We grew up understanding that we were always being looked at, the same way people maybe grow up knowing about dust in the Great Plains. When I was younger I spent a great deal of energy on being attractive, and that was a part of it, too. But what really magnetizes men to me is not beauty. It is a certain kind of brokenness, one that men gave me in the first place.

I went to therapy for long enough to receive a broad genealogy of this damage, which is so common that it is a dumb cliché and which has never felt like an adequate explanation for why I went so far into the lower recesses of human experience. I was sensitive, and I grew up with anger in my home, and I felt uncomfortable, and I sought comfort. Is that all it took for my dominoes to tip, pushing a small and lonely girl with big feelings into a wild and damaged young woman who smelled good to bad men? When I was working, there were so many other girls exactly like me that we were unremarkable, the obvious malfunctions of our judgment and chemistry palpable to men, the cracks in us showing around the edges of our uneven smiles and too-set jaws.

Twenty years ago, the block of Eighth Street between Sixth Avenue and MacDougal was a mini shoe district, along with the three blocks to its east, the place you would go to buy knee-high Doc Martens or Luichiny platform wedges. It was also where some of the stripper stores were, the places you would go to buy a Lucite platform stiletto with a seven-inch heel, that sort of thing. It wasn't as seedy as Fourteenth Street, where the traffic runs both

ways and narrow roll-down gates cover stalls selling the cheapest
and largest suitcases you can find in the city, the ones you see duct-
taped together on the baggage carousels after one-way long-haul
flights—suitcases for moving, not vacationing. Eighth Street was
quieter, its buildings smaller and lower, and it felt then, as now,
distinctly like the Village of the eighties, an odd mash-up of the
quaint and the abject, the sublime and the disappointing.

There was a smoke shop on the corner and a pizza place with an
open storefront on the south side of the block, the kind with stand-
up tables and sweaty air. I always walked north on MacDougal
and cut west to Sixth when I walked out of my parents' apartment,
because there reliably were small clusters of men smoking cigarettes along the block, and I smoked but rarely had enough money
to feel cigarette-secure. In 1999 it wasn't much of a thing to bum
a cigarette—a pack of Camel Lights cost less than three dollars. A
young or pretty girl could always have one just for the asking, and
I was both, and I knew it, so I asked, a lot.

I was walking across Eighth Street when I first met Cliff, the biker
who brought me into sex work. It was the middle of the afternoon.

"You're a very beautiful girl," he barked at me as I walked past
him. "You need a job?" I was high on pills and weak with starvation, a common scenario for me in those days, wearing a tiny
white dress I had shoplifted from the children's section at Diesel.

Cliff was far from a looker, but still, I stopped and let him talk
to me. He had good patter—he had honed it, I later learned, over
the years he spent picking up college students and pretty young
drug addicts on various downtown corners. *Recruiting*, he called
it. He told me that he was a photographer, that I had a special look,
that he had a good eye. He didn't fawn over me like men on the

street usually did; instead, he flattered while acting unaffected, as if he didn't really want anything from me. It was entry-level pickup artist tactics, but I was a kid, and my radar was set to home toward danger rather than away, so I stopped to talk, something that I knew better than to do but did anyway. It wasn't that I didn't understand that he was trying to game me—I wasn't oblivious to the goals of men. I stopped because I was curious about everything untoward and outré, and letting myself get plucked off the street by a camo- and leather-clad biker sounded, at the very least, like the beginning of a good story. I didn't understand what kind of business he had, but I took his card and called him a couple days later.

I dialed his number on my giant Nokia cell phone from my tiny bedroom in my parents' apartment on Washington Square. When he answered I realized my heart was beating high in my throat. He told me to meet him the following day at the McDonald's on Delancey, which seemed like the exact place you would pick to meet someone who you intended to dismember later in the evening. I considered not showing up. But even though I didn't understand exactly what Cliff's business was, I knew it had something to do with the intersection of sex and money, and I was interested in both those things: separately, but especially together. I was naive enough to never have heard of an S/M dungeon, though I surely knew what a dominatrix was. I had grown up blocks away from the Christopher Street sex shop strip, store after store selling cheap PVC outfits and whips and dildos and plastic handcuffs. I had already taught myself how to use sex transactionally. Though I hadn't yet received actual currency, I had figured out that I could move more easily through the world by flirting or having sex with people who had things I wanted, like drugs or alcohol or VIP passes.

To grow up in New York is to become aware of your own existence at the same pace and intensity at which it is reflected back at you. I learned who I was from the men of Manhattan, one hiss, comment, whistle, and free cigarette at a time. I learned that I had value, that I could get what I wanted, but that my value decreased the moment I made eye contact or opened my mouth to speak. The space between stuck-up cunt and too-eager beaver is cramped and precarious, but I had learned to occupy it deftly by the time I could walk in heels. I was ready to start working.

Me, Too?

The word *trafficked* is tossed around a lot by journalists and anti–sex work organizations. *Trafficking* is a legal term, meaning "the recruitment, harboring, transportation, provision, obtaining, patronizing, or soliciting of a person for the purpose of a commercial sex act, in which the commercial sex act is induced by force, fraud, or coercion, or in which the person induced to perform such act has not attained 18 years of age."

Traffic is also just a word, a transitive verb meaning to trade or to barter. In the dictionary its meaning is diffuse—you can traffic in oranges or three-piece suits or all-weather tires—but what it usually means when we use it is *someone stole that girl.* The girl who is trafficked is fundamentally good: an unequivocal victim, perhaps coerced, perhaps snatched in the night, small and delicate, easily hidden in the trunk of a car, likely to have five fingerprint bruises on her biceps. She is not interested in money or sex, and at heart she is a child. She is the pursued, always, and if she has complicity in her state of having been trafficked, it is naivete, perhaps accompanied, at worst, by a desperate need for love and protection.

The word *whore* is also tossed around a lot in American English, often with numb ubiquity. It is used so often as vague metaphorical referent that when I stop and think, I realize I have heard it used more than once by a professor during a lecture. You can be a fame whore, a media whore, an attention whore, and on and on. A whore, in the popular imagination, is someone whose primary personality trait is desire and who lacks the amount of shame we have collectively designated for the unabashed pursuit of desire's satisfaction. To be a whore is different than being ambitious, because if you are ambitious, you are using calculated effort and manipulation to get something you want that you then hold on to with mastery; while if you are a whore, you are spending a fast-depreciating resource on whimsical desires. A whore is someone who has allowed their ambition to parade around naked, and whose ambition itself is of the wrong, short-sighted variety.

In her book *Playing the Whore*, journalist and retired sex worker Melissa Gira Grant unpacks the words we use for sex workers, noting that "The person we call 'the prostitute,' contrary to her honorific as a member of 'the world's oldest profession,' hasn't actually been around very long. The word is young, and at first it didn't confer identity." Other than as the wry reclaiming of a slur, I don't personally know any sex workers who self-identify as prostitutes. There is violence embedded in the word itself, a sense of being misread and defined by a carceral force that doesn't well understand us or what we are doing.

"The word *whore* is older," Gira Grant continues. "There were countless people whose lives prior to the word's invention were later reduced by historians to the word *whore*, though their activities certainly varied."

By 1999 I was, if we are splitting hairs, both trafficked and a whore. I did not self-identify as either at the time, and neither feels quite true, even now, but both pass a fact check. I was seventeen years old, exchanging sex acts for money six nights a week, accompanying my "manager" across state lines on the back of his Harley when the whim struck him. I would never have thought of myself as trafficked because I never felt physically compelled to work—I was never threatened, not exactly, not in a *I'm locking you in the basement in shackles* kind of way, though there were guns, and knives, and a degree of surveillance that might reasonably be called stalking. But I arrived at work each night of my own free will, taking two trains to get there, ringing the buzzer to be let up. The proverbial gun was not to my head. I did not feel like a victim of anything, let alone a crime, which is telling of the ways exploitative men wield power over vulnerable girls: using our egos and our grandiosity as bits and spurs. The most prideful girls are the easiest horses to break. I wouldn't have called myself a whore, either, or even a sex worker, because I wasn't doing full-service work, not then. No one stuck their dick in me, and that seemed like the critical distinction, even though the bag of garbage the biker took out at the end of every night was full of wadded-up crumples of paper towel, sodden with rubbing alcohol and lubricant and semen.

It is a breathtaking (and I don't believe incidental) loophole of the American legal system that in most states, a minor can at once be legally considered both the victim and the perpetrator of the crime of selling sexual acts. According to Department of Justice records from 2019, in that year, 290 minors were arrested in the United States for "prostitution and commercialized vice." Forty of those children were between ten and fourteen years old.

In the eye of the state, if you accept money for sex acts, you are at once in need of the state's protection, and a criminal, out there wrecking homes. "We are using the policeman's eye when we can't see a sex worker as anything but his or her work, as an object to control," Gira Grant reminds us. "It's not just a carceral eye; it's a sexual eye."

I worried a lot about getting arrested when I was working. More so in the beginning, when the illegality of what I did for money was less normalized to me, and when it was more illegal because of my age. I turned eighteen just a few months after Cliff put me to work as a dominatrix, and any victimhood I could have claimed expired with that birthday. I didn't understand the precise legal consequences of being caught doing sex work, as a minor or otherwise, and the buzz of anxiety about all the bad and worse possibilities was with me at all times. Would I have gone to jail? My clients? The biker? The leaseholder of the office suite-cum-dungeon where my coworkers and I picked up the phone chirping "Artistic Innovations"?

In 2008, the year I started trying to quit sex work, there was a sea change in New York. For decades—as long as anyone I knew could remember, even the oldest old-timers of my clients—the cops didn't care about S/M businesses. What we were doing as professional dominatrixes occurred in a gray area wherein the premise of the businesses wasn't exactly illegal (we were considered performers) but much of what we did behind closed doors was. Both the large commercial dungeons with staffs of girls, like the one where I worked for the biker when I was seventeen, and the private independent studios like the one I ran toward the end of my working life, were, as a rule, ignored by law enforcement. But we all knew that what we were doing was prostitution, in legal terms, and was in violation of too many health codes to enumerate. There was also the constant specter of client death, and in 2008 it almost happened to one of our cohort, too flashy for the rest of us to avoid spatter burns.

At the very same dungeon where I had first started working, in the shadow of the Empire State Building, a girl tied a rope around a man's neck and dressed him in heels and stood him on a chair. At some point she left the room, and the rope slipped, or the heels slipped, or he slipped, and he couldn't breathe, and she wasn't there, and he very nearly died.

Okay. I want to say that she was very bad at the job of being a dominatrix, and also at the job of being a human. Both of those things are true, but truthfully I wasn't much better when I was young and habitually high on cocaine and also sometimes on ketamine and/or drunk—not exactly in a good state to keep tabs on the aliveness of a large and vulnerable body.

After that client, a professor, was rushed to the hospital and spent several days in a coma, the *New York Post* couldn't resist headlines like "HANGY SPANKY." No one will ever really know if it was causative or correlative, but right afterward, girls started getting arrested at dungeons in Manhattan, charged with prostitution. Commercial and private dungeons were raided by police in very *Law & Order*–feeling scenes: girls marched into squad cars in handcuffs, still in heels.

Sex Workers of the World, Unite!

It was during the series of community meetings that popped up in response to the dungeon raids that I first considered the possibility that I was a prostitute and asked myself what that word meant. I had always understood that I worked in the sex industry—that was the biker's turn of phrase, one I adopted and repeated without much analysis. I mean, of course. Men paid me unreasonable sums of money, by the hour, for various activities of mind and body that ultimately resulted in their orgasm. My work clothes were lingerie and rubber suits and minimum-six-inch heels, so, yes, I knew I worked in the sex industry. I hadn't yet related the term *sex worker* to myself, though, and I don't think I would have accepted it if someone had put it on me. Even though I dabbled in more traditional sex work, what I did as a pro domme seemed somehow more rarified, more empowered, and less, well, hooker-y than what I sometimes did with men I met on Craigslist, who would pay me for intercourse, blow jobs, hand jobs, or to look at me naked.

I didn't know exactly why I took those appointments. They didn't always pay better than my work as a domme, where I was able to set my own boundaries and charge a premium rate based on the reputation I had cultivated. I think that after a while, working in S/M had become so rote that I wanted to experience something that felt even more outré. It wasn't danger I was chasing, exactly, but an increased intensity of experience, something even less governable and farther from the kind of society my parents lived in.

S/M clients are so different from what we called "straight" or vanilla clients—far more likely to be obsequious and obedient, far less likely, in my experience, to get demanding or aggressive. The straight clients, who sought escorts, were men at their worst: lonely, petulant, and flakey, always ready to argue about cost. And unlike at the dungeon, I couldn't just hit them and tell them to act better. I had to create and participate in a much more delicate dynamic, one in which the men and I juggled the power in the room, each working against each other to meet our own needs but beholden to the other one to stop the whole charade from falling to the floor.

I was an excellent domme but terrible at the business of escorting. In S/M I could play a role and maintain my heavily policed boundaries by force, but when I had to be something closer to just myself and the ask was to be sweetly assertive? Much like in my personal life, I couldn't do it. I was prideful and a people pleaser, unwilling to argue about money or to assert any boundaries. The straight clients walked all over me, sensing my discomfort in talking about money and my strong urge to avoid interpersonal discord.

At my dungeon I did everything I could to convince myself it was a real job: I had business cards, a website, an accountant. When I took those off-label Craigslist appointments, though, I never presented myself as a professional, always as a dabbling civilian. My biggest fear when I met those men was not getting murdered or even running into a friend of my father's, but rather running into someone who recognized me as a domme. Working in the S/M niche of the sex industry, the work culture had trained us to think of ourselves as better than other kinds of sex workers. We told the men what to do, they licked the soles of our boots. Other girls gave blow jobs. Even though I was secretly also one of those "other girls," the existence of this constructed hierarchy was an easy sell, and I am now ashamed of how eagerly I digested the stigma that told me I could think of my fellow sex workers the same way the rest of the world thought of me.

"There is no one sex industry," Gira Grant explains. "Escorting, street hustling, hostessing, stripping, performing sex for videos and webcams—the range of labor makes speaking of just one feel inadequate." If I'd had her words to give structure to my experiences at the time, perhaps I would have better understood what I was doing. It just seemed like sex jobs were the ones I could get: the barriers to entry were less than zero. Being young and pretty in New York City made it easier to get a sex job than a waitressing gig. Later, after I quit working for the biker but before I started my own S/M business, I worked briefly as a cam girl and appeared in print pornography. This work seemed as unremarkable to me as I imagine raking leaves or having a paper route would have felt to some imaginary young person in more wholesome circumstances.

I wouldn't have said I was a sex worker, though I so very clearly was. I didn't feel a sense of better-than, I just didn't have a good word for what I was doing. Even now, I use the word *hooker* with a strong sense of ownership—like, you can't say that about me, but with a tinge of something not unrelated to pride I do say it about myself, retroactively. Carol Leigh, the activist and writer who worked as Scarlet Harlot and is credited with inventing the term *sex work*, wrote that the name she gave to the labor she was performing "acknowledges the work we do rather than defines us by our status. After many years of activism as a prostitute, struggling with increasing stigma and ostracism from the main-stream feminist movement, I remember the term 'sex work' and how powerful it felt to, at last, have a word for this work that is not a euphemism."

When the community meetings started, I saw for the first time a large group of S/M professionals, in daylight, together. Unlike the parties, where sex workers and civilians mingled and all genders were represented, this room was all women, and we were all work-ing. I knew many of them, but from sessions and parties and their websites, where everyone was shiny and lipsticked. Here, people wore jeans, came barefaced, had flat shoes on. A woman who I only knew by her dominatrix name identified herself as a lawyer and introduced someone from Legal Aid, who gave us a rundown on what to do should we find ourselves arrested.

I was well on my way out by then, going to school for metal-work, still not clear why I should quit domming but so uncomfort-able in my life that any kind of rattling of habits seemed worth a shot. I had taken my website down, dismissed most of my clients, and gone to renting hourly space at a private studio in West Chel-sea. I wanted to quit, but also I didn't. I kept three regulars who paid my bills and didn't demand much mental or physical band-width. I thought about cutting them off, too, but I had barely ever made money outside of sex work and I didn't know how I would support myself.

The community meeting was the first time I was exposed to organizing. I had a few working friends who were into what I thought of as "political stuff"—who worked with Sex Workers Outreach Project (SWOP), Sex Workers Action New yorK (SWANK), and grassroots groups that would go on to become the Red Umbrella Project. I didn't really understand what those friends were doing, even though I directly benefited from the community-building work they did. Their "political stuff" seemed separate from me, something I didn't need and didn't have anything I could offer to. I had a lot of privilege as a sex worker. I am white, I'd come from private schooling, I only ever worked "indoors" (meaning never on the street or in cars, where every risk that comes with sex work is dramatically increased), and I took nearly all of it for granted. Because I didn't consider myself to be participating in labor that was inherently political—and because it hadn't yet dawned on me that *all* labor is inherently political—I thought my "political" friends were doing something like going to grad school, which they also did, and I thought of all their non-working pursuits as utterly out of my spheres of reference.

I took the frightening uptick in police presence in what had been our safe little corner of the sex industry as another reason to get out. I had a very "yikes for them" feeling about everyone—including my friends—who chose to stay, to roll the dice and increase screening protocols and keep working. I didn't judge them for their choice to stay with sex work for the long term, but I questioned its viability, even as I knew that if the raids had happened earlier in my career, there is no question I would have continued working as they did.

I wonder, often, how my life would have changed if I'd been one of the girls click-clacking into a squad car, into a police station, the side of my face and my legal name on the cover of the *New York Post*. New York media loves shaming whores. I wonder how my life would have changed if one of my clients had died, perhaps the man so old I worried he would just keel over, who paid me so extravagantly that I wouldn't refuse him—thirteen or fifteen hundred dollars left in a messy pile of hundreds, and that just my tip. Or any of the others with their poppers and Viagra and cocaine: so vulnerable, all of us.

DEPRECIATIONS

TUCSON, MAY 2020, 97°
QUARANTINE WEEK 10, GESTATIONAL WEEK 27

Summer hasn't officially started yet, but in Arizona the temperature has already spiked to nearly one hundred degrees and it is already so hot that it is difficult to think about anything else. I look with trepidation at the following week's report and see a high of one hundred and four.

On a sweltering morning, I go walking with my friend Lucy. We mean to go at eight but don't leave until eight thirty, which is late in the solar timeline of a desert morning. When I get back home my gray shirt is patched with dark sweat under my breasts and armpits. I drink three glasses of water, one after the other, filling a fourth with magnesium powder to try to keep my electrolytes in order. N and I are in the middle of slowly moving out of our tiny apartment and into a bigger house, and I have disassembled all our furniture to the point that there is nowhere to sit except the mattress and the toilet and the floor. I hack a piece of leftover rib-eye steak into vaguely bite-size pieces and crumple down onto the ground. My body feels faint and trembly, some combination of hunger and thirst and low blood sugar and heat and pregnancy and not enough sleep. I eat the steak out of the container, cold, and guzzle the magnesium drink, hoping for a sensation of groundedness in my body that does not come. I am so tired, though I woke up just two hours ago.

Today, this is okay. I am hungry so I eat, I am thirsty so I drink, I would have slept more if I'd had the time. There is no satisfaction in hurting or depriving myself. I feel like I can't properly breathe, bound in the high waist of my leggings, my belly needing more room for expansion than the compression fabric affords it, so I strip them off when I finish the steak. I turn the air-conditioning up and sit on the mattress, waiting for the calories and salt and oxygen to fortify me.

In the midday sunlight of our empty bedroom I can see everything on my limbs: all the scars, even the ones faded or covered by my tattoos, their edges familiar to me because I remember the small violences that left them behind. On the front of my thigh, the worst of them, a patch of white keloid slash marks left by razor blades and kitchen knives and one fantastically dull sword from my friend Dahlia's collection of antique weaponry. On the soft meat inside the other thigh, the whisper of burns Dean left me with paper clips and cigarette lighters and stove gas. I know on the flesh of my ass there is a similar one, etched with a knife during a moment of acquiescence, long faded but once bearing his initials, the same kind of mark you put on a cow before you let her go low unattended in a field. Underneath the bright tattoos splattered around my arms there are more scars: horizontal slash marks, small speckled circles the precise circumference of a Camel Light.

I used to feel self-conscious of these scars—maybe because they used to be more visible, and maybe because the second and third acts of my life hadn't yet unfolded enough to counterweigh the senseless violences of the first. I felt made of scars, literal and otherwise, the walking wounded, a never-sealed rupture, a bag of need and dysfunction. When I felt that way it made sense—though the logic now seems flawed—that I would continue quietly hurting myself. Because I did not yet understand that pain was not a good long-term management tool for my feelings, it appeared I needed a cold blade or a hungry belly or a long rough run on a perhaps-broken heel to find some measure of peace within the hurricane of my selfhood.

The morning when N and I are meant to move our furniture to the new house, I am so tired I can barely rouse myself. I force myself up as early as I can to finish packing, after four hours' sleep. I have pregnancy insomnia and grad school deadlines, and I know I need to do better than this for my body but I also accept that life sometimes includes long periods of rest followed by the need to get a lot of tasks done in a short amount of time. I tape up the last boxes of our clothes and belongings and together we go to pick up a U-Haul truck. N's friend meets us at our apartment and the two of them move everything. I carry couch pillows and guard the truck, a job that I suspect is not altogether necessary but that N asks me to do and I gratefully accept. I cannot, with my protruding belly, reliably hold on to one end of a couch or a book-shelf, and this truth and the reality of my dependence make me uncomfortable, so it is a relief to sidestep them. It's not just that my muscles have weakened; they have, but I am still stronger than a lot of women my size, thanks to the years of training that preceded my pregnancy. It's that the geometry and physics of my body have changed: I can lift a box, but I have nowhere on my body to rest it. My sore swollen breasts and wildly expanded belly now take up the space where the box would rest. So many of the movements and positions my body is accustomed to no longer work: I cannot recline and rest my laptop on my body, cannot wash dishes with-out hunching my shoulders, cannot lift a barbell from ground to overhead, cannot easily hop-twist in and out of my truck.

I hate not being useful, but I also quietly love being cared for and the thrilling danger of my dependence. I watch N go up and down the staircase to our apartment, returning with dresser, couch, table, desk, bookshelf, bed. It is one hundred and one degrees and slow beads of sweat drip out of his hairline toward his beard. His shirt goes dark with sweat in the center of his chest. Some people walk by and I feel irrationally proud that somehow I have man-aged to deserve this beautiful man schlepping my furniture in the Arizona heat, that somehow I have managed to become so loved.

No one has ever helped me move before. I've moved alone, always, which has been made easier by not having much stuff and by being recklessly stubborn enough to do things like push a queen-size mattress up five flights of brownstone stairs, solo. I feel guilty and grateful at the same time. When I drive him to the airport at six thirty the next morning after we have slept on the floor surrounded by unassembled furniture under the inadequate cool of the ceiling fan because the air-conditioning isn't working at the new house, I tell myself that I will unpack everything before he gets home from his work trip, that in the four days I have until he comes back home, I will have the house cozy and comfortable and not full of tasks. I am committed, but foggy on details.

At the new house, our bedroom is flooded with light streaming through the large sliding glass doors, barely softened by the blinds. The bathroom has a huge mirror wall where I can see myself from the thighs up, and I put my full-length outfit-check mirror in the corner. In the brightness, naked, I really see myself for the first time since becoming pregnant, in full light, at full length. I am briefly horrified. My legs, in particular, are squat and lumpy, thigh backs pocked with cellulite, my ass and thighs running into each other without much discernment. My hips look sloppy where they used to look taut. I remember clearly loving the part of my body where the sides of my underwear would lie smooth across my hip-bones, tendons and muscles visible, a lean clean place. Now everything is sort of smushed together, my hip is my leg is my belly is my ass. The sides of my underwear have rolled up alongside my hips, probably because I have outgrown them.

I have been waddling around our apartment as close to naked as possible for months—clothes don't feel good, everything is wrongly constricting or baggily chafing. I cut the bottoms off a few tank tops and wear them cropped with my belly out, no elastic anything to cut into my newly pliant flesh. It had not occurred to me to question or critique my body. I knew, of course, that it looked different, but the smaller awful details were obscured by lighting and denial and concern with more important things. I take a moment, now, in front of the mirror, really looking, really seeing. I force myself to stop parting myself out into a list of complaints, to look instead at the curve of my belly and breasts, which I love, to appreciate that my body is now all softness and slope. I say *You look great* out loud, because it seems like something I should say to myself. It doesn't feel true. I wonder how N has been looking at me. He has shown no signs, I don't think, of seeing me differently, though I don't know how that is possible. The moment passes and I throw on one of his tank tops, which fits me like a dress, and leave the bedroom to unpack some more boxes.

It was breathtaking, for a moment, to feel the heft of my self-loathing, and to remember that I used to walk around with that, all of it, the full weight, at most hours of all days. I was beautiful when I felt that way about myself, too—beautiful in the conventional way I was trained by culture to value, tiny and pale and delicate and young, my hair long and thick, my skin flush with twenty-year-old collagen, my body not yet tattooed. I was so pretty that I hardly had to pay for anything. Men fell over themselves to give me drinks, invitations, bumps of cocaine, business cards, taxis they had hailed in the rain. Yet I felt so ugly on some days that I could not bear to leave the house, especially not in Manhattan, where every outing includes a verbal appraisal of what is or is not working about your appearance, and I fantasized at night about slicing slabs of flesh off my body with a chef's knife. I wanted to be small, smaller, as small as possible. I did not want to disappear. I wanted to be seen for my smallness, admired for my fortitude and style. I chain smoked and dressed exclusively in outfits I shoplifted from Barney's Co-op and was, in ways I could not appreciate until later when I became something else, a quintessential New York girl.

Now, I'm not sure what I am. The conviction that my body—its beauty and its ugliness, its states of being and of disrepair—is who and what *I* am feels wobblier. For a moment it occurs to me that if N can love me like this—and I mean really see and love me, not just look past it—that must mean more than being loved for being thin or fit or beautiful. The logic fades fast like a hologram. I grasp for its pixels as it goes, but I can't hold on.

I am alone for four days in our new house while N is in Vegas coaching a UFC fight. Las Vegas is closed to tourists for quarantine, and he sends me pictures of himself running on the empty strip, doing plyometrics on the lip of the Bellagio fountain. I miss him, and also this quiet time with myself and the baby is nice.

Our new neighborhood is nearly silent in the mornings, just the round sounds of mourning doves punctuating the stillness. At the apartment, there was the noise of loud traffic and often people screaming on the street early in the morning, which are sounds I am deeply adjusted to from growing up in Manhattan, so stillness really strikes me. Quiet is always a new sound, no matter how many years I spend away from New York.

I am bone tired from unpacking and assembling furniture, more tired than I can remember ever being from working out, though this is probably a failure of memory. My feet have a hard throb from walking back and forth over the Saltillo tile all day with fifteen extra pounds on my body. I want to sleep but I cannot: pregnancy insomnia is the body's way of preparing for the months and years of sleep deprivation to follow, and mine has manifested as early morning waking no matter how late I stay up the night before. I wonder why my body is acting like it doesn't remember that I am already very familiar with sleep deprivation, why it is being coy and pretending it forgets ten years of chaotic drug addiction and more years after that of being so mentally unwell and swirled up in compulsion that sleep was a distant idea. I am comforted, oddly, by knowing this body can, if it really has to, run on two hours of rest and chewing gum and coffee, that it has been proven able to do pointless battles with itself and survive.

I don't want to think about our baby this way—as an experience of lack or trauma or stress. I want only to think of our baby as a new friend, a very high-maintenance one, perhaps, but a tiny friend, the person I am closest to, half made of my favorite person in the entire world. I feel myself closing up when people talk about how hard parenting is, how obnoxious their kids can be (followed, always, by some version of *But I'd die for them!*), how much they have lost themselves. It's not that I think it will be easier for me, for us. The weight of it all feels clear. I do not expect raising our baby to be simple, or neat. I do hope, though, that suffering and personal disintegration will be optional. N is not like that with his son—doesn't carry him as a weight, doesn't appear to suffer for his parenthood. He enjoys him and honors his personality as it unfolds and changes and develops. I have never once heard him talk about parenthood as a chore, though he works harder at it than anyone I know. And for my part, I understand better than most people how to accept unacceptable weight, how to carry it as if it has always been a part of me, how to get cozy in discomfort.

I clean and unpack compulsively for the entire time N is away, through exhaustion and lower back pain and feet that ache so loud I start walking funny. I do not eat a proper meal for days—I am acting unhinged. I know he will not care at all if he comes home and finds the boxes right where we left them, the mattress still on the floor. But I want to finish everything, to make the house nice and comfortable and free of chores. I want to do something for us besides being a baby incubator, something tangible and material, some load of work taken off his back.

My nose is steadily streaming thin clear mucous and my eyes are swollen and itchy. I have never before had allergies, but some combination of pregnancy and poor air quality and Tucson tree pollen has turned me into a sneezy, leaky mess. I sweep a huge load of mesquite beans and palo verde buds from the patio at the new house and when I go inside I am covered with their dust, my hair smelling botanical, my nose pouring straight water.

The connection point between my belly and my hips is streaked with a deep ache, ligaments deep in my body pulling at themselves, growing painfully longer. I am so hungry that my mouth and jaw feel odd from the absence of food, as if they have lost track of what their work is.

I am wearing a filthy slashed-apart tank top and a pair of soft shorts that are now several sizes too small, my hair piled in a tangled knot on top of my head, my face streaked with dirt and shiny with sweat. I take a shower, scrub at my blackened feet with a rough stone, wash the front of my hair, and slather myself in coconut oil. The midday sun floods the bathroom as I stand before the mirror, seeing myself, making myself not look away.

Since becoming pregnant my once-glorious eyelashes have mostly fallen out, bald spots have appeared in my eyebrows, and I've developed patches of rosacea on the apples of my cheeks. Because of the quarantine, I haven't needed to dress for work in months. I cannot recall the last time I felt beautiful or pulled together or like a viable human woman. I have relished the sloth of allowing my beauty to deteriorate, but it eats at me at the same time, watching my stock fall one ungroomed eyebrow at a time.

N's fighter wins his Vegas fight in just over three minutes, a triumphant victory I watch on my grainy laptop streaming ESPN, squinting to see N leaning on the outside of the octagonal cage, his beautiful face obscured by a UFC-regulation face mask. His fighter's opponent taps almost as soon as he finds himself in a guillotine choke, back pressed against the mat, neck cranked upward, head twisted around its axis. I watch the fight as I sneeze and ache, my heavy body draped over a large U-shaped pillow, thinking about pain and ambition and the fundamental inability of anyone, even someone whose very profession it is, to accurately predict their ability to withstand pain in the future.

It is easy, always, to watch the fights and think that whoever taps or falls or fails to advance could have done better—they could have taken more pain, shown more bravery, eaten more punches. Half the people in the crowd at any given fight are, at any time, voicing such sentiments, so much so that the unathletic UFC fan—the "couch coach"—giving frustrated direction to their fighter is a whole genre of meme. Watching someone else endure is a two-dimensional experience, fundamentally unrelated to actually enduring with your own body.

I cover the red splotches on my face with concealer, and for the first time in months I spread some makeup across my face. I groom my eyebrows and fill them in with some brown pomade, put two coats of the most dramatic mascara I own on my stubby lashes. This is all it takes—I recognize myself again. My body still feels sloppy and my face is missing the angles that used to make it noticeable, but I feel pretty, not haggard, and it is a relief bigger than I could have imagined.

SCALES OF HARDNESS

To weld steel, you strike an electric arc by scratch-tapping an electrode on the surface of the metal. It's a similar motion to striking a match, and like a match, if it's done right—not too fast, not too slow, your movement neither rough nor timid—a small burst of heat and light erupts. That's the arc. Then a tiny lake of metal turns molten where the electrode meets it. That's the puddle. To look at the light, you need the dark-tinted glass of a welding mask to prevent corneal flash burn—an eyeball sunburn. To weld, you push or pull the puddle with the electrode, guiding it into a bead. If welded correctly the cooled bead will join the two pieces of material into one, and the joint where they once were separate will be stronger than either piece was on its own.

never understood how people got careers, or even jobs. At twenty-three, I was freshly sober and extremely messy, and I had only ever worked in sceney downtown restaurants and the sex industry. I had happened into everything in my life, and I wanted, more than anything, to become tough.

I had never known a metalworker before I met Dean. He was a builder, specializing in architectural metalwork. "Welding is the vocation of criminals," he had once told me, through teeth that were holding a long thin copper-dipped filler rod for a TIG (tungsten inert gas) welder. He was leaning against a rusty acetylene tank with one eye squeezed shut, holding a machinist's square up to the steel angle clamped to his worktable. "Makes it a nightmare to find good guys. If you learned how, you'd definitely get work."

Welding itself is a delicate operation. If you strip away the affectations and accessories of grizzled manliness, the manual movements of holding an arc and running a bead are closer to knitting than to anything else. You need a careful eye, a steady hand, and a stubborn perfectionism that will compel you to spend thirty minutes grinding out a weld that took an hour to complete if you think there might be an air bubble trapped inside.

Dean's Brooklyn metal shop was dark, grimy, and cluttered, the thick steel slab tables covered in greasy clamps and metal shavings. My heels crunched when I walked across the floor. I had never been in a place like that before. I loved it.

On one of the many days when I stopped by his shop to deliver lunch, I casually asked him what he thought about me learning how to weld, fully expecting derision.

"You should do it," he said, without hesitating. "I could help you get started."

Flush with the fantasy of reinvention, when I left I was already carrying myself in an imperceptibly different way. My shoulders were a hair straighter, my body a tiny bit less languid. I hadn't done anything yet, but the idea of recreating myself with proper armor made me feel stronger. I thought that if I learned to weld, Dean would see me differently. He had always treated me like a silly person, someone undeserving of respect.

"Just ignore her," he would say to his guys when I hung around the shop while they were working. I wanted his approval so badly that I decided I would remake myself, and I would do so in a way that would make it impossible for him to scoff at me. My dominatrix job was his richest source of material for why I was frivolous and slutty. Metalwork was tough, honest, and serious. In my head, the math worked. Even though I literally punched and kicked men for a living, being a domme had rarely made me feel tough. The *idea* of it was, but my lived experience didn't match. If I could be a welder, I thought, I would finally feel hard enough—for Dean, and maybe even for myself.

Hardness is the ability of a material to resist friction, abrasion, and indentation—to resist change brought by force. It is not a fundamental physical property, but rather a characteristic. In metrology, the scientific study of measurement, there are six hardness scales. Each one has a specific application— the Vickers scale, for example, is a microhardness test, used to measure the hardness of small, thin materials like ceramic or composite, while the Shore scale is used on polymers and thermoplastics. On the Mohs scale of mineral hardness, the kind of carbon steel used on buildings is scored at four Mohs units.

*Ice—the kind you might drink—scores a one and a half, while
a diamond—the kind you might wear—gets a ten.*

I got my first metal job by walking in and asking if I could work for free. I don't know exactly what the guys there thought of me, but Dean had asked his buddy Rob to hire me as a favor, and Rob said okay, and just like that, I had a job. Kind of.

Rob's eponymous shop, Ferra Design, was amazing. They did fabrication work similar to what Dean did, wildly expensive custom metalwork for restaurants featured in *Time Out New York* and townhouses occupied by *Forbes* listers, beautiful heavy things that would survive an apocalypse. On my first day, Rob walked me around the shop, showing me the lathe, the band saws, the German welding tables, the racks and racks of material, the jobs in process. It looked like a combination shipyard and sculpture studio. I was dazzled.

Ferra was the most truthful place I have ever been involved with. The shop's slogan was "If you demand the highest quality, expect to pay the highest price," and there was no fudging of anything. Precision was an almost religious code for everyone who worked there, from the two old-school Brooklynites who founded the company to the Pratt Institute graduates who worked for them as fabricators and project managers. My job was to do the low-skill repetitive work, like sanding, to free up the real guys to do the high-skill operations. While mine were the most rote of the tasks available, requiring vastly fewer skills than the welding, fabricating, and computer-navigated water jetting the other shop workers were doing, perfection was no less important. I had literally never done anything like that before. Sure, the operations themselves were new, but that wasn't the shocking part. They were simple chores anyone with decent focus and hand–eye coordination could do. The hard part was the commitment to excellence.

In metalwork, perfection is relative to function. "Good enough" for a decorative fence is different than "good enough" for structural steel beams on a high-rise building, which is different than "good enough" for an aerospace turbine. Perfection, as a philosophical ideal, is inherently unachievable, but technology and industry edge ever closer to its possibility. A perfect weld has zero porosity, full penetration, and no cracks or undercut. If you're working on buildings, which I often was later in my career, an inspector from the Department of Buildings comes around with a portable X-ray machine to check your welds for imperfections from the inside, but the truth is that when you are welding, you can *feel* perfection.

At Ferra, it was humbling when my cuts on the band saw came out a full eighth of an inch off, when there were visible scratches peeking out of the material I had sanded, when a hole I drilled was off center, when I left a jagged burr with the grinding wheel. And because I had no experience with being humbled, it felt humiliating. It is impossible to tell lies with steel, so I hid the pieces I mis-cut in the scrap pile behind the saw and I burned with shame when my work was checked, knowing it was subpar. I wanted to do better, but the only things standing in the way were focus and effort, and I genuinely didn't know how to give them.

I had lived my whole life like a raft in a current, following whatever path offered the least resistance, so I didn't know how to steer, how to drop anchor, how to row. It was easy to call anything difficult impossible and float away from it—at least it always had been. But I really wanted this job. I had a deep and immediate respect for Rob and the guys I worked with at the shop. Every one of them was palpably brilliant, intensely driven, cool, and surprisingly gentle. No one was ever creepy. They were each generous with their time and talent, teaching me different ways to do things, giving me lessons and space to practice. I had happened into a warehouse of MENSA-meets-Bunyan big brothers.

Matt, a project manager at the shop, taught me how to handle metal with respect, the way you might handle a large animal. Unlike other materials, metal does not respond to force—only to technique. One morning, before we were headed out to a jobsite, Matt handed me a piece of precisely bent steel to cut.

"Take an inch off with the grinder," Matt told me. "I scribed the line for you."

I clamped the awkward piece to the edge of the fabrication table and started burning through it with the grinder. The problem was that I had never cut something so thick with a grinder before. It wasn't until I was about a quarter through the cut that I saw how jagged and irregular it was. I could tell it was fucked but I didn't know how to fix it. Matt came up behind me just as I was letting the gravity of my mistake sink in.

"Wow," he said. "That looks like shit, huh?" Matt is so mellow and even tempered that he can say things like that without them feeling personal. Everything is *we* and everything is *how can we fix it, how can we do it better.* He believes in the work, and in collaboration. I, on the other hand, believed in shame, which I felt. It did look like shit.

"Let me show you a better way," he said. "And then we can figure out how to fix that side." He took the grinder out of my hand and started cutting from the other side. He went over the scribed line, just barely scoring it along the whole length of the cut, making a long shallow groove. He kept going over and over the groove until it was all the way through the material, and it looked perfect, like a machine had made it. The cut was straight, true, square, and precisely where it was supposed to be.

"That works better, yeah?" he said, kindly. I nodded, red in the face with gratitude and embarrassment. He dragged the cord of the TIG welder over to the table and meticulously filled in the gouges I had created, then ran a grinding stone over the steel until the whole piece was perfect again.

Once I had been at Ferra for a couple months, Matt started staying late to give me welding lessons. He would sit next to me at the fabrication table with a mask on so he could watch my work, a little pile of scrap metal between us.

Weld the two rusty ones together.
Fill the gap.
Keep the heat low.
Drop one bead.

I kept welding, doing these wax-on wax-off exercises, torch in one hand, rod in the other. I was used to men helping me or doing me favors with explicit ulterior motives, and Matt didn't appear to have one. I couldn't see the angle and I was willing to believe there wasn't one. Matt was generous and he liked teaching; he knew a lot and was willing to pass it on. I wanted him to feel like the time he was investing in me was worthwhile—like I deserved it. I sensed from him that he believed in something about me, that he thought I was worth the training, and that my hard work mattered even when I was clumsy.

> *To test the hardness of a material, you take an object of known hardness, like a ball of tungsten or a spheroconical diamond indenter, press it into the material, and see how much pressure the material can stand before sustaining damage. In industry, these tests are performed under extraordinarily specific and tightly controlled conditions. The point of all this testing is to ascertain the conditions under which a material will fail. When you are building a high-rise tower, or a bridge, or the components of a car's braking system, the differences between too hard, not hard enough, and just right are the differences between architecture and casualty.*

I loved working at Ferra, and for the first time in my entire life I was proud of what I was doing for money. Rob, who had changed the trajectory of my life by giving me the job, had graciously started paying me by my second week of work there. But it was barely enough money to pay rent, and I had kept a few dominatrix clients to bridge the gap between my car service and restaurant habits and my suddenly finite paycheck. Around the time I had asked Rob for work, I had also applied for a spot as an apprentice with one of the big New York City ironworkers' unions. There were so few available apprenticeships and the waiting period to see if you'd gotten one was so protracted I'd nearly forgotten about it, but one day when I was guzzling a coffee in the material storage alley outside the shop that served as our break area, I got a call from the union, telling me there was a spot for me in the apprentice class that would start in the fall.

The union job paid so much money, more than quadruple what I made at the shop, plus benefits. I liked money, and I had dropped out of college, which seemed like the only avenue to a well-paying job that didn't involve nudity and ejaculate, so I took the job, working as an apprentice ironworker for Local 580.

Ironwork was different from the kind of metalwork we did at Ferra. The work was bigger, heavier, less precise, and performed at heights on high-rise buildings. I didn't know how to do any of it. There are a lot of professional avenues for a welder to take, and when I used to tell people I was a welder, they would usually ask first if I was an artist, then if I made jewelry. It was hard, I think, for people to imagine a small young woman doing the kind of work I was doing, making things so big it took cranes to lift them. I spent most of my welding career working in architectural fabrication and installation: metalwork for buildings. Those jobs run the gamut from relatively cushy indoor operations like Ferra, making bespoke spiral stairs and fancy doors and other custom architectural features, to decidedly un-artsy construction welding, which is ironwork.

Ironwork takes place in the middle of the sky. Cranes raise great giant stabs of steel I-beams, and welders like me lean over urban abysses to weld joints that aren't accessible to anyone with reasonable fear of heights or death, in the bitter cold and the blistering heat. Ironwork, unsurprisingly, is men's work. It is heavy, dirty, and dangerous: one of the seven most dangerous jobs you can have, as measured by the Bureau of Labor Statistics. In the United States—the country where a presidential candidate once called for "more welders and less philosophers"—about 2 percent of ironworkers are women.

When I started my membership with Local 580, the union office told me to go to an address in Long Island City for a physical, height test, and drug test. All of this had to happen before I could go on a list to be placed at a job. When I arrived, I could tell from the group assembled out front that this job was going to be a far cry from Ferra. I was the only girl at Ferra, too, but the workplace culture was much less concerned with displays of masculinity. My bosses and coworkers had all gone through the Industrial Design program at Pratt Institute, where they learned as much about Richard Serra as they did about tensile strength and the drift capacity of steel. They were all craftsmen, artisans rather than construction workers, which created a distinctly different vibe.

As I walked up to the long line of men and took my place at the end, I tried to look at everyone without being obvious. I was afraid to be seen looking—it felt of paramount importance to appear cool, chill, and unaffected by my difference. I felt like a dumb little fancy pony in a group of Clydesdales. The men lined up with me were different from the Ferra guys—they were the exact type of guys that had been catcalling me as I walked down the street since I was thirteen. Big and boisterous, unafraid to take up space, talking loudly and swearing often. There were so many of them, one set of muscles after another, everyone dipping Skoal and talking shit with each other. I didn't see any other women.

Finally, the nurse called me into the medical trailer for my physical.

"Oh! Look at you!"

"Hi. I'm Margo." I could tell she was surprised to see a girl, and that she was wondering why the fuck I was trying to be a part of this thing, this man brother iron balls dick testosterone thing. I was wondering the same thing myself.

On the first day of apprentice school, which started before our job placements, the instructors explained the work line to us. We had to call to put our names and union book numbers on the list for jobs, and it was a first-come, first-served system. You sign up, and then you wait. While you're waiting, they told us, you have to be ready. You would get a call—The Call. You had to keep your tool bag packed and sitting by the door, your work clothes laid out like a firefighter's. You had to be rested and sober, with your phone bill paid and the ringer turned on, because you were going to get The Call one morning, maybe at seven but maybe at five, with an address you had to hightail it to that same morning.

I felt like I was going to vomit while receiving these instructions. Everything about the system seemed like it was set up for maximum stress, and I was so self-conscious and unsure of myself just being around those guys—being stared at for my conspicuous gender and talked at but not to—that I didn't feel like I had any more to give. I remembered feeling a similar way when I started working as a dominatrix, when I didn't know what I was doing and felt bored into by the stares of the men I was working for. In both spaces, I was young and green, thrust into an extreme circumstance by the wildness of my desire to feel tough. I thought if I acted a certain way—if I acted hard—I would become so. In a way, I was not wrong. It just took much longer than I expected, and by the time it happened, the veil of what I had once understood toughness to be had lifted and there wasn't much left for me to hold on to.

Toughness is a material's ability to absorb energy without rupturing or fracturing—that is, to resist strain while under stress. Tough material, like steel, is not easily cracked or broken. It is possible for a material to be hard but not tough—a diamond, for example, doesn't easily scratch but would shatter if you took a hammer to it—or tough but not hard, like the silk of the Darwin's bark spider, which is many times tougher than Kevlar.

As I waited for a call from the Local 580 job list, my anxiety got worse and worse. I would train as an apprentice for three years, working alongside the journeymen on jobsites for a percentage of their pay and attending apprentice school at night. I hadn't yet worked a day as an ironworker, but it didn't occur to me that it was okay to be inexperienced. Even though I was explicitly there to be trained, I felt like I had to arrive already knowing how to do everything, to make up for being a girl. The thought of showing up on some construction site with a giant group of men I had never met and seeing them look at me as a joke, a disappointment, some stupid girl when they had called for an ironworker, felt impossible. I could barely bring myself to think it through or imagine what it would look like. I didn't feel like I had enough armor to protect myself from this torturous self-consciousness, and my dread grew bigger and toothier with every day that passed without The Call.

My anxiety ratcheted up to a rolling boil of near panic, and I was scared of that feeling, because my coping mechanisms for anxiety had historically not been very good.

Knowing I would be heavily outmatched and outnumbered on a big union jobsite, and needing a task to channel my worrying into, I focused on trying to erase what remained of my outward femininity. My head was already shaved down to a #2, as it had been since before I started at Ferra. I laid out the outfit for my first day: two sports bras, dark Hanes tank top, oversize T-shirt, Carhartt vest, knit hat. Thick canvas double-knee Carhartt pants, two sizes too large. I wanted to vanish my body inside of them. I had bought a package of boy's briefs at Duane Reade, not because I was actually trying to pass as a boy, but because it felt important to build the new, genderless image of myself from the ground up. I laid a pair of those out too. I removed the small diamond studs I always wore in my ears. I clipped my nails to the quick. The whole process was a reverse drag, a self-conscious deleting of anything gendered female.

Nevertheless, I have never felt more girly than when I was first stared down by a gauntlet of fifteen hundred men on my way into work at six thirty in the morning. When I finally got called to a site, I made it there before the doors opened at seven, so they were all loitering outside smoking cigarettes under the scaffolds, men from every trade slurping roach coach coffees out of paper cups and waiting for the workday to begin. I didn't even look up at the building. Later, I would learn it was designed by Jean Nouvel, situated on the end of a block known as "Starchitect Row." There was a Gehry across the street, a Shigeru Ban down the block. Photographers from *Dwell* and *Architectural Digest* were constantly

holding up traffic by standing in the middle of the street to take
pictures. But all I saw was men.

"Hey, do you know where I could find Local 580? Or Marc
Rivera?" I said, dropping the name I'd been given on the phone
and trying not to look at any one of them. They all had hard hats
on, dinged up and plastered with stickers like a table in a punk
rock bar. My hard hat, brand new and as yet unworn, was all black
and had no stickers. It was clean and smooth and matte. I tried to
hide it behind my body.

"Yeah, the big guy, right? Likes to dance?"

"I'm not sure. Is this the way in?"

"Yeah miss, go right ahead in." I hated him for giving me permission to enter, for declaring that I needed permission, his, any.
For calling me *miss*. I realized how little any of my physical preparations had mattered. Shaved head and baggy clothes-ed or not, I
was a girl, and I was in a men's space, and none of my attempts to
perform masculinity offered much comfort.

I mumbled a thank you as I walked inside. I heard rau-
cous giddy laughter around a corner. A huge man toddled over
to me, with a smile so bright he reminded me of a child. He
looked kind.

"Are you Margo?" I nodded, upon discovering I was mute. "I'm
Marc! How you doin', chick?"

I liked Marc immediately, and my instinct was a good one. He
was safe, equal parts fun uncle and chatty pal. During the years
we would work together, he always treated me like a daughter, and
could reliably be found singing and laughing and spitting sun-
flower seed shells onto his belly. I needed someone to be nice to me
right at that moment, and he was perfect.

I worked for the local for five years, and on all but one of the construction sites I welded on, I was the only woman ironworker. Walking from the parking garage to the site at six thirty in the morning, the sidewalk was always a stream of neon green and safety orange, Red Wing boot prints in the dust outside the building. I looked for other girls, keeping my eyes carefully unfocused, my expression purposefully blank, but it was rare to see one, and the closer I got to the site, the smaller and more seen I felt, a small girl, a vague oddity, something in the way. In my local union of about twenty-five hundred members, I knew the names of the other five women by heart. *MargoNicoleMarilynJenMarleneJill.* No matter how good we were at welding, or how much we tried to blend with the men, we were all known, collectively and interchangeably, as "the girl."

There were women working at other trades on some of the jobsites. Riding the hoist in the morning, I'd catch a glimpse of a plumber with a long braid down her back, a steamfitter with skinny jeans tucked into her Red Wings, an electrician with red lipstick on under her hardhat. Not all the women tried to disappear into the cloud of testosterone like I did. Some of them asserted their femininity with their presentation. I found this mortifying and distanced myself from them. I didn't want to be part of some weird girl gang. I wanted to be one of the men.

Steel itself is closely linked to masculinity in the cultural imagination. The identity of the ironworker is thus deeply invested in a performative stereotype of masculinity—a strength that eclipses that of a regular man. "Men of Steel," as the hardhat stickers said. But what is inherently masculine about steel? Steel is hard and hard is strong, yes, but there are many harder materials out there, like rubies and diamonds, yet the jewelry industry is not, to my knowledge, rife with the kind of sloppy gendering that happens in the building trades. The culture of ironwork is obsessed with how tough you are, how fearless and strong, how well you can get it done. The guys were always bellowing stuff like *Git 'er done,* little hypermasculine pep talks on the way into the hoist in the morning—stuff that to me was like a cartoon parody of Big Tough Man World. The thing that made it more than just parody, however, was that the work *was* heavy and scary, difficult and strenuous. The performance of strength seemed redundant, because everyone *was* strong.

To be strong is to resist damage. There are two measures of the strength of a material. Yield strength measures the amount of force required to initiate the deformation of the material—to start bending or warping it. The yield strength of a material represents the point up to which it can remain itself, unchanged by the forces of the world. Tensile strength is a measurement of the force required to break a material. Some materials have high yield strength but low tensile strength, which means they can resist a great deal of force, but once the force alters them, they can't hang on for very long. Concrete is such a material; it is very difficult to initiate damage in concrete, but once you've gotten into it with a jackhammer, it flies easily apart in shards and chunks. A material with high tensile strength can exist with structural integrity even under the pressure of damaging forces. The tensile strength of structural steel is about seventeen times that of human skin.

The physical discomforts of metalworking cannot be overstated. In the ten years I worked as a welder, I was lucky to never suffer any serious injury, but I gained a body-wide collection of small second-degree burns and knife slices, multiple instances of frostbite, more smashed toes and fingertips than I can recall, and a toxic accumulation of manganese in my blood that has yet to dissipate. I fell into a hole carrying hundreds of pounds of copper welding lead, took a spinning shard of drill bit to the cheek, broke my thumb in a vise. I burned my hair, my thighs, my forearms, my neck.

The first time I hurt myself welding wasn't serious, but it was so painful that I went mute, too stunned by the sensation of being burned to let out a noise. I was TIG welding at a fabrication table at Ferra, holding my torch in my right hand and my rod, the long thin stick of copper-coated metal I was melting, drop by drop, into the groove I was welding, in my left. Unlike other types of welding, the tungsten inert gas welding process separates the electrode and the filler material, and thus requires both hands plus a foot pedal to control the amperage from the welding machine. If you need to hold or adjust anything while you're working, there aren't many good options. I had gotten into the bad habit of pushing the cold end of the rod against my body to choke up on it when it started to run down—an amateur's move, I was about to discover.

I finished the bead I was working on, clicked my hood up, and sat up straight, trying to uncrunch my back. Without thinking or looking, I pushed the rod into my chest to get set up for my next weld and immediately felt a pain that was shocking in the way of a hornet sting, piercing and cruelly concentrated on a tiny area of the body. I had somehow flipped the rod and pressed the red-hot side into myself.

TIG rod is skinny—this one was probably a sixteenth of an inch, just twice the diameter of the metal in a paper clip. I usually wore a standard welder's suede jacket, but it was hot that day, and I was stupidly wearing a T-shirt. The rod burned straight through the shirt, through the spandex of my sports bra, and deep into the soft flesh at the very bottom of my breast. I was so startled by the sensation that I froze, my mind a few beats behind my body, the breath gone from my lungs, my mouth filled with cold saliva. I didn't understand what had happened for a moment that felt like a very long time, and when I did, I was overwhelmed with an embarrassment that distracted me from the pain as it spread across my chest and into my shoulders. The rod went in so far, melting the spandex of the bra into the depth of the wound, that the tiny lump and scar has held to this day, looking like a bullet wound from a doll-size gun.

Every winter that I worked on-site, I swore to myself it would be the last one, my boots stuffed with hand-warming packs, my belly full of cayenne pepper pills to raise my body temperature, a hair dryer in my tool bag to keep frostbite at bay. Later, when I was working on cranes in the Honolulu summer, I learned about another host of discomforts, smearing thick zinc on every visible piece of skin and chugging electrolytes to keep from passing out as I sweated through my thick welding jacket. All of which is to say, the money was good, but I earned it.

After a while, some of the men warmed up to me. I worked hard, and they saw it. When the foremen came around asking who wanted to stay late for overtime, I always said "I will." The ones

I felt most comfortable with were dads—men who knew how to take care. John, who meticulously planned his daughter's birthday parties; Patrick, who saved up to get his kid horseback riding lessons. I was careful not to talk much about my personal life, because it was important to me that they saw me as a neutral entity and never pondered my gender or sexuality. My biggest fear, workwise, was that I would be thought of and treated as weak, sexual, or vulnerable in any way.

The men, however, talked about everything: their families, their work gripes, their injuries, the jobs they had worked on. The ones I steered clear of talked performatively about sex, while others made a big show of editing their stories—"Watch your mouth," they would say, reminding each other that I was there, that they were not alone. I was equally uncomfortable with both versions of special treatment, but because I didn't talk much, they talked to fill the silences. My hope was that they would treat me like a daughter—if not theirs, then at least someone's.

Of the men who were fathers, none of them wanted their daughters doing our job. Some brought their sons into the business, but not girls. It was too rough, too heavy, too cold, too dangerous. That's what they *said*. They saved money to send their daughters to college, to give them lives that didn't include frostbite, spatter burns, and zinc poisoning.

Underpinning all these awkward dynamics was a palpable element of territorialism I never stopped feeling in my decade of metalworking. *Why are you here?* they would ask, sometimes snarky, sometimes playful, occasionally with genuine curiosity, but it wasn't a question, it was the drawing of a boundary. Some asked me straight out—especially after they found out that I was

smart, that I had gone to private school, that my dad was a lawyer. *Why?*

Why not? I always shot back, short and flip, intended to silence.
None of us was trying to start a dialogue, we were just testing
which trees to piss on. The truth was, I wondered the same thing
all the time.

By the time I graduated my apprenticeship, I finally cut my
last ties to sex work. I'd long since deleted my dominatrix website and let go of my dungeon lease, but I'd kept my last remaining client for my first few years on the jobsites, seeing him at his
apartment once a week for an hour, during which I gave him an
extremely lackluster session, often still dressed in my welding
clothes. I had wanted to stop seeing him the whole time and once
I started working for the union, I could technically afford to, but I
had been afraid—afraid to lose the connection to easy money, but
more than that, afraid to fully step into the new version of myself
I'd built from scratch. Going from the jobsite to those sessions
made me feel like the ultimate fraud, as if all my performances
of toughness were just a farce to cover up who I really was, which
was something dishonest and malformed that didn't fit anywhere.
When I made journeyman, I finally told that last client I couldn't
see him any longer and erased his number from my phone, but I
felt permanently stained by overlapping sex work with my new
career. So when the men asked me *Why are you here,* I heard it as
an accusation, an assertion that I didn't deserve to be in the world
of hard, honest labor.

*Ductility and malleability are the measure of a material's
ability to deform under, respectively, tensile and compressive*

stresses without fracturing. Loosely speaking, tensile is pulling and compressive is squeezing. Tensile stress is the resistance of an object to a force that could tear it apart. Think force under tension, like the chain on a bicycle, the string on a guitar, or the cables on a suspension bridge. A material with high ductility can easily accommodate pulling forces. Compressive stress is just what it sounds like, and the quality of malleability is the measure of a material's ability to stay intact in the face of compression—think about gold, the most malleable of all the metals, which can be easily marred by the compressive force of the human jaw.

Welding is an acquirable skill. You do it long enough, and you get good at it, or at least better. I was shitty at welding for a while when I started at Ferra, but I started to get better quickly, because the fabrication table was a place where I could press away all my anxieties and preoccupations. It's reductive to compare everything to meditation—meditation is its own thing—but there was a mind–body state created by the repetition and the embodiment of focus that did something good for my brain. As an apprentice, I did whatever tasks I was assigned. My favorite type of work was to be left alone with a repetitive task, tightening a seemingly endless series of bolts or welding the same series of seams all day long.

I worked for the union during the year, and in the summers I would take off and go up to the farm with Dean. We worked on the house, did farm chores and projects, and sometimes when he was running a metal job down in the city, he'd hire me for a day or two to help with the delivery or installation. Dean's jobs were strictly hierarchical. He dispensed enough instruction to serve the job, but no more. Since I'd gotten my union job, things had shifted a bit between us, but barely. He still mocked my work, but with a different angle: now, his material was that unions were for lazy idiots. He made fun of my coworkers and my tasks and, by extension, my whole existence. I was bitterly disappointed that I had devoted my whole self to being worthy of his esteem but had somehow still failed. Occasionally, though, it would be different. There were a few things I had learned how to do that were valuable to him, like installing material at heights, and when he needed those skills, he treated me like someone who had something he wanted. Even though I knew it wouldn't last, I relished the feeling so much that I would do anything to earn it, climbing up any sketchy ladder he pointed to, ready always to risk my safety and self-respect.

I wanted to be partners with him—in business and in everything else—but he never saw me as more than a resource, someone he could extract from. He was willing to mentor me in a limited capacity in the trade and the business, but I would never be his partner, I would only be his employee. At one point, shortly after I had completed my union apprenticeship and earned my journeyman ironworker's card, we agreed that I would move upstate to the farm and work for him on a big job he had taken. I was excited. I thought that if I did a good enough job, maybe it could be the start of a new dynamic for us, professional or otherwise.

Working for Dean on an ongoing basis was a fucking mess, it turned out. He'd built a huge, beautiful, glass-walled shop on the property upstate, yards away from the house, so we never had to leave. We never had to leave. I became tethered to the property in a way that felt so claustrophobic I would invent errands to go on simply to get a breath of air I didn't have to share with him. As a boss, he was critical, manipulative, and demanding, a far cry from the mentorship I had gotten from Matt and Ferra or the training I'd received on my ironworker crew. With Dean, nothing was good enough, and if anything went wrong, he flashed immediately to anger.

"What did you do to this?" I remember him demanding about a structural steel frame I had welded, a task he had left for me to do alone. It wasn't a complicated element, and I had done an okay job, but I hadn't clamped the tube steel well enough to the table and when I had run the beads along the seams to connect them, the heat had pulled and warped the steel, putting a subtle but distinct twist in the whole piece where it was meant to be perfectly flat. On-site, we would bolt the frame to the roof we were working on, where it would serve as support for the series of extremely expensive aluminum trellises we had fabricated for the owner of an NFL team. No one would ever see the frame, and I was pretty sure my mistake wasn't big enough to cause a structural issue.

We had been working fifteen hours a day for weeks to finish the job, and there is always a degree of triaging that takes place on big jobs. Not everything can be both perfect and on time. I had thought the small mistake would be okay—I knew it wasn't perfect, but I thought it was not that bad. But Dean had fifteen years of experience on me, and he had a much better eye—a boss's eye, tuned always on mistakes and imperfections.

"This is all fucked up, what did you do? I thought this was good to go on the truck?" His voice was rising. The frame was sitting on the welding table, waiting for us to load it. He pulled the corner

up, trueing it with his eye and finding it lacking, looking mad-
der by the second. I felt my face getting hot, my throat starting to
close. It was nighttime, and the rest of the guys had gone home.
We were alone in the shop.

"I'm sorry, I thought it was good to go. I didn't realize it had
warped so much." He wasn't listening, so I trailed off. He dropped
the corner of the frame back onto the table, letting it slam with
a loud metal clang, and stalked out of the shop. I knew there was
no time to start the frame over, or to cut it up and fix it. We were
due in the city to install the job in the morning. I didn't know
what to do—whether I should follow him into the house and apologize, keep packing the truck, or just sit there and wait for him to
come back and yell at me. In my body there was a strong urge to
run, destination unimportant, just away. I fought it, and watched
him go into the house. I was cold and dirty and wanted to change
before the five-hour drive, but I was afraid of tangling with him,
so I stayed in the shop and loaded the tools in the truck, feeling so
ashamed I could barely stand it. When he came back to the shop,
we loaded the frame and the rest of the material together without
speaking and drove to the city in a caravan, he in his big dually
pickup, me following in my smaller truck, grateful for the separa-
tion. The next day, at the jobsite, we installed the frame. I waited
for it not to fit, perched on the edge of panic that the warp I had
fabricated into it would cause a catastrophic installation issue. But
we dropped it into place, and it went in just fine. It wasn't perfect,
but it wasn't trash—it was good enough. I wanted to ask Dean
why he had yelled at me, why he had stressed perfection in an
instance where it wasn't necessary, why he was so intolerant of my

errors, why he had to terrorize me over them instead of teaching me. But I wasn't stupid, and I knew those questions would only lead to more of the same, and I didn't want to get yelled at anymore, so I said nothing.

A couple years later, I started working as a freelance subcontractor, outside of the union. I knew the work and the business well enough that I didn't want to be told when I was allowed to have a cup of coffee or take a bathroom break anymore. That's what I told myself, and it was true. But the other, bigger truth was that I didn't want to be "the girl" anymore. I was a card-carrying journeyman ironworker, licensed to weld and erect steel in every United State and southern Canada. I had graduated at the top of my apprentice class and earned a prestigious award from the Department of Buildings. I had worked on Nouvels, Gehrys, Calatravas, the new Freedom Tower. I had seen them at their most unpretty, and I had, in some small way, been part of what made them stand. But my name on-site, always, was still The Girl.

Every new man that came on my crew would give me his coffee order, assuming I was the apprentice. And every morning, every season, I still put on two sports bras and two shirts because I was afraid of my nipples showing through my clothes. I had grown my hair out, so I covered it with a bandana, secretly jealous of my one female coworker who brushed out her waist-length hair in the shanty every afternoon, giving no fucks. The work it took to maintain my image of desexualized indifference was heavy, always, and I understood that no matter how good I got at the job, it might never go away.

If you know how to work with metal, you can play materi-
als god and change some of its elemental properties. Take steel
and temper it correctly, and you're left with a material that is
stronger and tougher, with improved ductility and decreased
brittleness. Tempering steel is simple: heat it to the appropri-
ate temperature for the alloy you're working with, which will
be very high but below the melting point, and hold it at that
temperature for about two hours. Then, quench it in cool water
or oil and heat it slowly at a more moderate temperature. Tem-
pering makes steel more useful for the tasks of daily living.
When you've completed those steps, you'll have the kind of
metal that is appropriate for a knife blade, a hand tool, or an
automotive part.

When I left New York to move to Hawai'i, I took a small bag
of welding tools with me. I had a plan to work for my friend Elko
on his farm, doing manual labor and managing his crew of workers. I knew metalwork was the most efficient way for me to make
money, but I didn't know how to arrive in a new place and get a
metal job. Even though I had been welding for almost a decade
and carried nearly every license a welder could have, I still felt
unqualified—not because I was new, but because I was a girl.

In liberal New York, the unions have rules about gender equity,
and there was such a palpable fear of sexual harassment lawsuits
that a lot of the guys policed each other's language or steered clear
of me altogether. That didn't exactly make things easy, but at least
I knew that as a union member I would have the same priority
for placement on the work list as any other member. In Hawai'i, I

didn't know how it would work. I put my name on the work list for the local union out of Honolulu as a "boomer," or traveling member from another local, and I waited. And waited. And waited. In New York, you could call in to the work list line and an automated voice would read you your number on the list. Everything was transparent, in large part because of a discrimination lawsuit that a group of Black union members had successfully brought against the local some years back. It was a good, functional system. In Honolulu, you had to call the front office and talk to a person, and they would only confirm that your name was on the list.

Working on Elko's farm, where I exchanged my labor for rent on the tiny shed I lived in without plumbing or electricity, I wondered if I really needed to go back—to face it all again, all the men, all the explaining, all the proving of myself. I fed animals and planted seeds and weeded gardens during the day. I barely had enough income to put gas in my truck, but Elko was kind and treated me with respect. I could work in a tank top, no bra.

In the summer of 2015, I finally started getting hired for union welding jobs in Honolulu, thanks to some low-key political manipulations that were performed on my behalf by a man I was sleeping with. I worked on crane installations and structural steel under the hot Pacific sun, and in the middle of the summer I got on a fast-paced overtime job on a building that was behind schedule. The ambient temperature of the site registered ninety-four degrees. I was put to work alone, welding connection points on the I-beams. The decking crew was right behind me, laying down sheets of reflective metal that created a mirror effect. The sun and the decking blasted my eyes and skin with blinding UV rays in every possible position.

On my fourth day, a piece of molten slag pinged off the decking and burned its way through my pants, settling into the soft flesh of my inner thigh. It burned a hole the size of a pencil eraser in my skin and wafted a charred-hot-dog smell through the haze of iron welding fumes. I knew from experience that it was futile to try to dig the slag out of my clothes. I was wearing a thick suede welding jacket, gauntlet gloves, and a safety harness with two thirty-pound bolt bags attached to it, and I was straddling an I-beam several levels up the building. Undressing quickly was not an option.

I had spent so much time, by then, training myself to disassociate from pain—physical, emotional, whatever—that it was no longer just a trick I could perform, it was the way I always was. I didn't know how to have a normal reaction to anything. Before I felt the pain, I felt the shut-down, the cementing of my face and severing of the connections between my experience and my affect. I had gotten so good at masking that the mask had become my face. I didn't quite feel what was happening—it's more that the sensations were being logged for me to experience later, in a safe and private space, where I could be alone and unharden myself. But in another way, okay, yes, I felt everything.

The pain started as a white-hot laser point and pressed outward, at once targeted and diffuse, my entire leg feeling as if it was being disintegrated, or perhaps microwaved. As the seconds passed and I sat, frozen, my welding hood thankfully still down over my face, my gloved hands clenching the flanges of the beam so hard my fingers would later ache, I felt the pain pulse and wave, moving into and through my body, settling in my low belly with a heavy wash of nausea. I felt as if I might fall off the beam, even though it was wide and I had my feet tucked into its lower flanges as if they were in stirrups. The pain from the burn and the lack of vision under the hood made me feel like I had been spun in a washing machine and had lost orientation to earth and sky. When I am in great pain I become very still—a scared animal's instinct to freeze, or maybe the illogical notion that I can somehow evade the pain that way—so I had to tell myself consciously to move, first to unclench one of my hands from the beam, then to push my hood up, letting the bright sun stream into my eyes.

I felt as if I had been hit. I threw up a little bit into my mouth, swallowed it, and picked up my torch, which was dangling in the air. I had been sitting, absorbing the pain of the burn, for long enough that the tip of my rod had gone cold. I took a few more minutes, wishing I had a cigarette, feeling the post-orgasm feeling of the pain receding, feeling myself reenter my own body. Then I clicked my helmet back down, struck an arc, and kept welding.

My body bears an erratic constellation of scars from similar incidents. All welders' bodies do. They are concentrated on the forearms, wrists, neck, clavicle, tops of the ankles, and backs of the hands. All the gaps between garments where sizzling metal finds its way in. There are also errant burn scars I am unable to explain: left breast, top of right thigh. Belly. When hot slag falls inside or burns through layers of bulky protective gear and settles in for a slow, deep sear into flesh, it leaves marks that seem to be permanent.

Straddling the I-beam above the Honolulu skyline—acres of shipping containers to my right, an expanse of blue and palm trees to my left, the scents of plumeria and the sweet-bread bakery down the road mixing with the oily chemical tang of hot steel—I clenched my eyes and mouth closed as I worked, waiting for the pain to recede. If metalwork has taught me anything, it is how to absorb pain without reacting. How to be hard.

When I look at my body I see its evidence all over me, the wreckage hardness has left behind. My arms, which once were slim and fit for spaghetti straps and delicate bracelets, are thick from a decade of lifting welders and steel. The funny bulge between my ribs on the left side, where my intercostal muscles tore while I was lifting a bundle of stainless-steel handrail and never quite healed. My ripped-up shoulder, which for years could not lift so much as a mascara wand without several audible clicks and a sear of pain. All the burns, the scars, the fucked-up toenail that didn't grow back right after I dropped a pressure plate on it when I was an apprentice. My eyes, full of microscopic particulate metal. My lungs, which spent a decade huffing fumes "known to cause cancer in the state of California," filling with acetylene and welding flux, clouds of metal, until they hacked up black phlegm with little spots of blood.

When we speak colloquially of hardness, toughness, and strength, we often conflate the three, but to pull apart the definitions is to understand that there are many ways to resist the forces of change and harm, and many circumstances in which one and not another is called for. I went to metal for the same reasons I went everywhere else: to try to rebuild myself as a creature impervious to damage. To live with the reality that I am made of a soft center, that I am delicate and sensitive and utterly available for harm at every moment of every day, was unbearable to me, and so I tried to disprove this fundamental fact of existence. I tried so hard, until I had to admit to myself that it was impossible, that there is no way to be a human without being vulnerable to hurt. To be a soft thing was my greatest fear, and greatest shame, but it was true all along—the great awakening, for me, was not in becoming ever harder, tougher, stronger. It was, instead, in becoming brave enough to look my softness in the eye.

The night after I burned my thigh on the beam, I made a quiet decision. Sitting on the lip of a friend's bathtub with Bactine and silver sulfadiazine and big rolls of gauze spread out around me, I decided I was done. What I had bought myself with my banged-up body and my endlessly swollen and deflated ego was a sense of access and self-assurance that was mine to keep. I had found the place for which I was most ill-suited out of all the possible places I could have inserted myself. I had persevered through the hard stares and the namelessness, through being called "sweetheart" and "the girl" and being treated like a novelty and a moron. I had hardened myself, and now my work was through.

WADDLE LIKE A CAGE FIGHTER

TUCSON, MAY 2020, 104°
QUARANTINE WEEK 11, GESTATIONAL WEEK 28

I get sad when I sit too long indoors without movement or sun. N brings Thai pads home from the dojo and gently coaxes me to the park during the short hour when the sun is descending, a semi-respite from the bright hot heat. I haven't hit pads in months, not since before we found out about the baby, because we didn't want to tell anyone yet and I was afraid someone in N's muay Thai class would teep me. A teep is a front kick followed through with a hard push of the toes, generally administered directly to the belly, infinitely more violent and painful than its graceful appearance indicates. One of N's friends teeped me once, play-fully, when we were sort of silly half sparring, with probably 10 percent of his actual power, and I peed myself a little bit and fell directly onto my ass. So I stopped going to N's class back in January, and then quarantine began, and in the interim my body has grown stiff and swollen.

In the park, the grass is as green as it ever gets in Tucson, low on the hard-packed ground. Soon, as the heat progresses, this grass will be dead. Parts have died already, scuffed into dusty turf by dog paws and sneakers and bicycle treads. We find a decent patch of green, safe in the shade of two big trees, and sit down to warm up.

My body feels alien, as if parts that should be connected to each other have come—not loose exactly, but like their threads have worn thin or their bolts have begun to shear. My sacrum feels like a bag of hardware, glancing against the rest of my lower back but not gaining purchase. I am not in pain, exactly, but I am full of strange feelings.

N shows me how to sit and arrange my legs in a geometric pattern on the grass, one forward of my torso and one behind it, making ninety-degree angles with my thighs and calves, and then how to stretch one leg long and rotate my hip through its capsule. It is a small movement, just one leg moving a few inches, back and forth, back and forth, grooving the nerves in the hip socket, reminding my body its pieces are still connected.

I don't understand nearly as much body science as N knows, so in my mind, a funny feeling in my back means that something is wrong with . . . my back. *Knee bone connected to the thigh bone* is the level of orthopedic knowledge that feels logical to me. But I trust him, now. After two years of explaining my pains and watching as he really listens, then skeptically moving some seemingly unrelated part of my body and feeling my pain slip away like pixels into a dark screen, I really trust him. I first arrived at his gym with so many of my parts feeling broken, misaligned, irreparably damaged from years of misuse. I thought my body was ruined, and I thought this because I had been told so, and because it felt so. It was my hip and my shoulder and my back, yes, but other, slipperier parts too, pathways and connective tissues between body and mind, between movement and feeling, between sensation and emotion. I thought *I* was ruined, and not just orthopedically, and when he told me otherwise I thought he was mistaken. But today my shoulder doesn't click and my hip doesn't scream and the only reason my back feels funny is that it is swelling and loosening to house a tiny person, the tiny person I thought my body was too broken to conceive.

We start warming up, shadowboxing. My body feels creaky and unfamiliar, like a stiff puffy jacket that was stored in a small box, ill-fitting and unwieldy. The grass under my sneakers feels grippy and uneven, my hips and shoulders disconnected from each other, my legs heavy and slow to move. Without the three-minute-round clock N always runs during his class, the time stretches on, feeling interminable, the seconds failing to add up to minutes, my body wanting to stop.

N shows me how to hold my fist to punch without a glove, since we haven't brought any. *Protect your thumb*, he tells me, showing me how to curl it around my suddenly-tiny-looking fist, but my brain can't take anything in, can't absorb or recall. I am hot and tired and pregnant and probably a little bit quarantine-depressed. I know I need to move my body in one of the rough sweaty ways that makes it feel its animalness, but I have a powerful desire to just sit down on the ground.

In this feeling, N is the only person who I can hear talking to me. His deep steady voice cuts persistently through the wild static in my head. I can keep going.

We finish warming up, N fiercely shadowboxing the way real fighters do, nothing lackadaisical about it, his brow lowering as his head settles into his neck and shoulders, his body coiling into a different thing than it was a moment ago when we were sitting on the grass as people. I halfheartedly throw some punches, wanting to save my limited energy for hitting the pads and, without him to focus on, self-conscious of my round body moving awkwardly through space. I wish I didn't feel this way, because truly I have never been prouder of my body, but I can't shake the feeling of being a spectacle.

N picks up the big black leather Thai pads and slides his forearms through their straps. He holds one up for me to punch. One large bead of sweat slides slowly down his temple, past the dark line where his hair, long and pulled back tight into a curly knot, meets his face, past the wispy coils of escaping ringlets, toward the swooping mustache and thick black beard he has grown since we met. I love his face so much that something crumples inside me when I look straight at him. I sometimes have to blink or look away to avoid tearing up. I didn't know, before him, that I could love this much. I didn't know my heart was this big, that I had the capacity for anything but criticism and demand. I didn't know I could look at someone and really see them, their humanness, their imperfectness, and love *that* rather than an idea of them that is necessarily disrupted by their true self. I didn't know I had any of this in me.

My body moves differently now, and each time I use it for a thing that used to feel a certain way there is a lag, a gap between my expectation of finding that old way and the new reality of how I now move through space. Actions that felt autonomic, that happened without a conscious process of *thought, intention, movement, action,* are now pulled apart into sequences. N holds the pads up for me to kick and I have to remember the steps: *Step out with my standing leg, toes angled away from the centerline of my body. Rotate my moving hip in its socket and raise my moving leg as I extend it, swinging it out and around. Pivot, at the same time, my standing leg, with my heel elevated and all my body's weight on the ball and toes of that foot. Kick through the pads, not just into them, as I continue to pivot my foot and rotate my hip.* He has taught me all these movements, slowly and purposefully, and while I have never gotten better than beginner level, there was a time last year, when my body was small and taut, when the kicks felt smoother and easier: a thing I was not great at but definitely knew how to do.

Now, I forget pieces. For the first five or seven kicks, my body moves too slowly through the layered sequence of movements to achieve the necessary simultaneity. N holds the pads up patiently as I reset myself and try again, offering me gentle reminders every few minutes. *Pivot on that foot. Kick through the pads.* I forget my self-consciousness, forget everything but my mounting exhaustion, which comes so fast these days that I am chasing my breath for almost the entire time we are working out. I am frustrated with myself for not being better—stronger, with greater endurance, crisper in my movements, in greater control of my body— but it is a fading feeling. I watch N's chest, trying to see where he will move next. I watch his face watching me. We don't make eye contact but we are focusing so intently on each other that it feels like some other kind of contact, something closer to touch than gaze. He holds the pads close to his body and parallel to the ground, signaling for my knee. I forget the movement we have drilled, and he reminds me: forearms stiff and parallel to each other, plant one in the crook of his elbow and one in the side of his neck, brace and pull forward against him, step into him and plant the knee up and forward, into what would be his belly if we were fighting. This practice is, for me, about exercise, and so it is easy to forget that these are all functional movements, the blocks, catches, parries, punches, elbows, kicks, and knees into the pads mimicking how a fighter would defend themself and attack an opponent.

I am so spent after ten or so minutes of hitting the pads that I drop to my knees on the grass and try to catch my ragged breath. I attempt to control it: seven seconds in, seven seconds out, the sequence that will most quickly kick on my body's parasympathetic nervous system response. The sound of my breath is rough and uneven, gasps of jagged air and moisture pushing through space.

I think, as I now do whenever I become conscious of my breathing, about labor. It is difficult to assume and maintain control of my breathing—its timing, its intensity, its depth, whether I am doing it at all—in the midst of intense effort, and one of my bigger downfalls as an athlete is a stubborn tendency to hold my breath when shit gets difficult. Every coach and trainer I've ever worked with has had to remind me, some sharp and censorious, some gentle like N, to breathe.

On the way home, my shadow looks big and lumbering. *Babe, am I waddling?* I ask N. He slows his step and walks behind me for a few beats before resting his hand on the crest of my butt. *Nah, babe, you're walking like Conor McGregor.*

IN THE CLINCH (I)

Violence

I n the back of a strip mall in northeast Tucson, the storefront entrance to Rise Combat Sports read FRIENDLY ATMO-SPHERE. Inside the gym, the walls were red-painted cinderblock, the air thick and clammy with perspiration and body heat. The amenities were few. This was a place of business: the business of tactical violence.

The group of mixed martial arts and muay Thai fighters who met to spar at eight o'clock on Thursday nights made small talk as they wrapped their hands and began to warm up, shadowboxing and hitting bags. I caught scraps of their conversations: *hip control, one-fifty, what are you walking around at, seventy-two.*

As the fighters settled into the rhythmic motions of punches, kicks, and elbows, I curled my legs underneath my body on the small piece of mat space I had staked out for myself on the perimeter of the sparring area. Some of the men were already soaked with perspiration, droplets splashing off their brows and dark wet spots spreading across the chests and underarms of their shirts. Josh Purcell, the fighter I was there to observe, hadn't started sweating yet.

Josh was one of N's fighters. I had been closely watching him train and spar with N as they prepared him for the tenth fight of his amateur muay Thai career. We were six weeks and three days out from the date when Josh would step over the top rope of a Thai boxing ring, touch gloved knuckles with an opponent, and fight until the time ran out, one of them became incapacitated, or the referee stopped the match. There was much work to be done in preparation: strength and conditioning, sparring with as wide a variety of partners as possible, drill after drill of tactical actions and reactions, and a weight cut that would slash twenty-five pounds from his already lean frame. These preparations made up what is known as the training camp: an intense, compressed period of time—Josh's camp was eight weeks long—in which a fighter is molded into the fittest, wisest, and most dangerous version of himself he can become.

N and Josh knew I was writing something about violence, and they had agreed to open their camp and fight up to my project. I was interested in what they were doing athletically because I was in pursuit of answers about sport and spirit and bodies and men. I didn't know exactly what I was looking to discover, but I had a feeling there were answers here, in these spaces of camaraderie and brutality.

We—it was they, the fighters, really, but I had tagged along, as unobtrusively as possible, or at least that was my hope—had traveled across town to Rise so Josh could spar with a bigger fighter in preparation for his fight. At 5 feet 11 inches, Josh was taller than any of the men in N's cadre of athletes, and in a sport where feet are flying at temples, this was significant.

Josh was a study in contrasts: the kind of guy people like to call a character. He authored a series of absurdist cartoons he exhibited, guerrilla art–style, in portable toilets around Tucson, but to peg him by his scruffy beard and his sleeve of tattoos as a hipster artist would be to miss the mark badly. He was a white rapper from Chicago with a heavy CrossFit habit who installed roll-down garage doors for a living, and when he wasn't cutting weight for a fight, he ate apples and peanut butter for breakfast every morning. In conversation, he asked questions more than he talked about himself, and read—accurately—as someone who would stop to help a stranger change a tire.

Even at rest, Josh emitted a low-pitched energetic restlessness. There was a certain quickness to him, something I had felt immediately when I met him. "I always had to be busy," he said of his life before fighting. "Too much leisure and I start to get itchy. I will get into trouble if I don't have something to do." When he spoke, he stared directly, his attention toeing the line between intent and aggressive.

Before there was muay Thai for Josh, there was skating, there was graffiti writing, there was rock climbing, there was Cross-Fit, each done at what can be fairly described as an extreme level. Before there was fighting in a ring, there was a different kind of fighting, too, the kind that found him in handcuffs at the age of twenty-two, looking down the barrel of a very different sort of life. In all those pursuits, there were the four elements that together populate an obsession for Josh: "danger, luck, skill, and being an idiot."

I identified the fighter Josh had come to spar with as soon as he stepped onto the mat. He was the largest man in the gym, taller than Josh by at least a few inches, broader and wider too. He wore flashy traditional Thai shorts—shiny black and gold silk emblazoned with tigers—and pulled on python-printed shin guards and padded headgear. Josh was dressed in board shorts and a somewhat ill-fitting black tank top. He put on shin guards—his were black, and one was held together with tape—but when the Rise trainer looked around the mat and barked for everyone to put on headgear, Josh shrugged and said, "I didn't bring any."

It wasn't that he was foolhardy. He didn't make the mistake of underestimating his opponent, or the potential for grave and amortized damage to his brain and body; that much was clear from the way his face settled into a mask of focus as soon as he pulled his gloves on.

Sparring, his stare went from intense to menacing. The first time I had seen him on the mat, my immediate thought, which came so fast I said it out loud without thinking, was *I wouldn't want to see him in a dark alley*, and after watching him train for several months, it felt like I could see him making calculations behind the blank wall of that stare.

I suspected that the more exposed he was, the higher the pressure was. The more he was challenged, the more focus and precision was demanded of him, and that demand was what Josh was there for. Winning a fight or besting an opponent was secondary to all of this. He wanted to win his fight, sure, but Josh's real reason for being in the ring was to spend time with the outer reaches of his own psyche.

The fighters broke into pairs: four on the mat, one in the MMA cage. I had a hard time deciding where to focus my attention. Josh's partner, the big man, was a strong fighter, with power in his kicks that I could feel from across the mat, but even to my eye his body lacked the speed and shark-like efficiency of Josh's. It was difficult for me to determine how much intensity each fighter was giving: this was not a fight, after all, just training, and the men shared a warm and respectful rapport. No one had come here to deliver a beatdown.

Shirtless, with a flushed face and his popsicle-red mouthguard visible between his lips, Josh looked terrifying. His shoulders shrugged up to meet his clean-shaven head; his vulnerable neck vanished in his fighter's stance. Gone was the easy smile he had walked in with; in its place was a deranged-looking grimace.

On the risers of the steel steps leading up to the MMA cage there were two warnings: NO SHOES IN THE CAGE and ENTER AT YOUR OWN RISK. N sprang up the steps and entered the cage with a smaller pro fighter named Casey and they began to spar, delivering complicated-looking series of kicks, punches, elbows, and knees, their compact bodies flowing and clashing into and away from each other. They circled each other like animals, and broke into quick grins when someone connected, a duet of admiration as much as a fight.

On the street, two small boys walked up to the storefront, inches away from the cage but separated by the glass. They stopped, transfixed, their mouths open, their eyes peeled wide. I went back to watching N and Casey, and several moves later, I glanced back outside and the boys were still there, still staring, the larger one in a bright green hoodie that ringed his face like a halo. He was perhaps having one of the pivotal moments of his young life, I realized, watching two men toy with violence in such a visibly playful manner.

I thought about how my father had reacted when I told him I was dating a fighter, that I was taking boxing classes myself. *It's just so violent,* he said, of mixed martial arts. *I can't watch it.* I thought about the people I knew—and there were plenty—who wouldn't watch fight sports because they were uncomfortable witnessing such brutality. I was deeply suspicious of this squeamishness; it felt conceptually similar to eating meat while maintaining horror at the thought of actually butchering animals. There was hypocrisy there, of course, but there was also something that to me felt more sinister: the idea that by refusing to look at certain spectacles, there can be moral cleanliness from the existence of violence.

We are a culture of euphemism and sanitation: of chicken fingers, of nipple pasties, of boneless breasts. We, too, are a culture of violence: of feedlots, of rape, of roughness systematically applied

to some while others clutch their pearls and say *I can't watch that.*
We lack hunger for truths about the violence we participate in. No
one wants to watch the whipping scene in *Roots*, nobody wants
to read exactly how Larry Nassar pushed his unwashed fingers
inside children's vaginas, nobody wants to see the glistening
organs of a freshly slaughtered pig. We want, instead, to cringe,
to look away, and to affirm our humanity for doing so even as we
claim ownership of land made fecund with slave labor, even as we
settle into La-Z-Boy chairs to watch the thrilling performances of
USA Gymnastics, even as we contentedly wipe bacon grease off
our chins.

The boys standing outside the glass will come to know violence,
most likely, if they hadn't already. They will meet it or witness
it in their homes, in their schools, in their relationships. "Every
day in America men are violent," the feminist cultural critic bell
hooks writes. "Their violence is deemed 'natural' by the psychol-
ogy of patriarchy, which insists that there is a biological connection between having a penis and the will to do violence."

I wonder what is meant, exactly, when we use the word *violence*: what bell hooks means, what I mean, what has been carried
through centuries of social evolution on the backs of three small
syllables. From the Middle Latin, *vim*: power, energy. The Latin,
vis: strength, especially as exercised against someone, also *viol-
entus*: vehement, forcible. When did the tint of unhinged sadism
grow to become the whole color of this word, which in today's English we understand to mean physical force intended to hurt, damage, or kill?

As N and Casey landed kicks and knees on each other's bodies, I
felt glad the boys outside were seeing their power, their energy. If

I had a son I would want him to see that strength can be exercised against someone—and we can keep calling it violence, because language is clumsy and leaves great breaches of approximation between shifting and complicated truths—without hatred, without fear, with brutality but without malice. I would want him to see and to know that there are healthy spaces for the call to roughness and body contact I believe lives inside the human animal, that here, in this cage, these men found a model for a different kind of roughness, a respectful violence that appears brutal, but that at its heart is truer and more honest than ways of being that wrap harm with politesse.

Impact

To prepare a Thai boxer for a fight is to receive much force. In a training session, Josh kicked N so hard he left a brownish-purple bruise the size of a butternut squash on the side of his thigh, despite the thick leather Thai pads and shin guards between their bodies. He elbowed him in the right eye socket, leaving another bruise behind, this one a ring of darker purple the size of a slice of peach.

N would bring his body to my home after these sessions, during which he held pads for Josh to punch, kick, knee, and elbow, N absorbing the force of the blows into his own body. He said little of the consequences of all that impact unless I probed, but I could somehow sense the reverberations of everything he had just sustained, vibrating off his body like song from a singing bowl.

To absorb violence, to commit violence: are they reciprocal actions, moving in a circle, or does the flow of effect move ever outward? Josh and N were more than athlete and coach; they were close friends.

Do you carry it with you? I asked Josh, about the rough treatment he must rain down on men he cares about to be ready to enter the ring.

"Someone has to be that person," he said—the person giving direction, holding the pads, and receiving the impact, that is— "But I try not to take that for granted. I try to take the things he's saying seriously, to not waste it, to make it as good an experience for him as possible."

That is the way of combat sport: to prepare for a fight, there is collateral damage not only to your own body, but to those of your sparring partners and coaches, too. The fighters accepted this truth as part of the unspoken contract they entered into when they trained together.

N, a third-generation martial artist, spent much of his younger life training to fight MMA until he was nearly paralyzed in a training accident when his partner spiked his head against the mat, compressing his neck and damaging his spine so badly that he had to recalibrate to a new normal in which coaching took the place of fighting. The health of his spine was hard-won, a decade-long project, and, I feared, precarious. It was sometimes difficult for me to watch Josh kick him.

When I saw N's body reverberate with the force it absorbed, I was torn. I was the person who loved him, loved his body, wanted his wellness and resilience and knew that the various parts of him would be better off in five, ten, thirty years if he never took another kick to the belly or another elbow to the face. But there was another part of me that was stronger, the part that wouldn't dare to wish a bridle on a wild horse, who saw in him generations of martial skill and pride, who knew that to fret about a man like him would be to fundamentally misunderstand who he is.

N has trained and coached Josh from his very first day practicing the traditional Thai kickboxing known as muay Thai, long before either of them knew Josh would eventually step into the competitive ring. Josh has never had another teacher, and in this way, Josh was N's, a fighter molded completely and only according to his design. Elusive by temperament as a combatant, Josh was most comfortable playing a game of evasion, ever slipping out of his opponent's range, using his fitness to his advantage as he moved inside and outside.

N didn't fight this way. He had a different instinct, one less evasive, stylistically incompatible with the desire to run or to hide. In raising Josh as a fighter, though, N decided that trying to alter his instinctive style—the personality of his fighting—would be counter to the project of making him the most powerful version of himself he could become. So his persona, his ringcraft, and his ethic were all layered onto that first, truest instinct: his fighter's heart.

In the three years that Josh had been fighting competitively, he took on nine fights, winning five. His very first competitive fight was in a tournament format, meaning that for as long as he won his fights, he would fight opponent after opponent with mere hours between bouts.

Against his first opponent, he experienced a phenomenon known as an adrenaline dump. Dreaded by fighters, soldiers, and cops, the adrenaline dump begins when a threat is perceived by the amygdala, which triggers the sympathetic nervous system to activate a sudden, intense release of adrenaline—this is commonly understood as "fight or flight response." If given time to recover in perceived safety, the body recalibrates and returns to normal. But if that threat signal continues to be triggered, the amygdala keeps leaning on the doorbell, overwhelming the body with cortisol and adrenaline and causing a series of nearly immobilizing aftereffects during which the body struggles to recover its functions.

By Josh's estimate, he felt thirty seconds of superhuman strength during his first fight: limitless in his power, impervious to pain. Then his body began to vibrate, and suddenly he was "watching the fight through the inside of a straw." This tunnel vision was accompanied by a bodily exhaustion that he had no comparison for. Though he won by judge's decision, he only watched the tape of the fight once, because he couldn't bear seeing himself in such a weakened state.

"It was a terrible experience," he told me, clearly frustrated with himself even in the recounting. "Everything took more effort than I had, I was truly giving 100 percent of my effort. It was not what I envisioned. It makes me cringe."

Sport fighting is, above all, a game: a bout between players, yes, but also, and perhaps primarily, a test of the self, of the successes and failures of the integration of physical prowess, emotional regulation, and tactical skills. Control of the body, control of the mind.

Contrary to what I might have thought before I came to know these men, there was a marked lack of sadism in the why and the how of their fighting.

"I don't fight because I'm trying to hurt people," Josh told me, sipping on herbal tea. "But I'm happy to beat the fuck out of my friends."

What did this mean, this cheerful enthusiasm for splitting the lips, bruising the ribs, and blacking the eye sockets of people we love? My friend Emma came to muay Thai class with me and kicked me so hard in the belly that I lost all my wind. She did this four times in six minutes, but after the class I felt no complicated emotions, only a clean exhaustion, love for her, and respect for the power of her legs.

I am a person who has hit and been hit under many convoluted and confusing circumstances: in bed, in ritual, in anger, in play; in fear, in desire, in boredom, in rage. Upon request, upon demand, without consent, in terror. I have struck and been struck by enough men enough times and enough ways to feel sure that there is nothing inherently bad or good about rough contact, that context and consent determine the value and consequence of such actions.

In her New Materialist essay on the physics and politics of touch, feminist scholar Karen Barad reminds us that "touch, for a physicist, is but an electromagnetic interaction." I am far from a physicist, but I have done enough experimenting with and on my own body to understand that what I am feeling is the meaning of a thing, not the essence of the thing itself. The story attached to a sensation alters my experience of it; this is why I once loved getting hit and choked in bed by a person I selected but I am afraid of being hit and choked by a stranger on the street. The electromagnetic interactions might be approximately the same, but the nature of the experience is altogether different, same-looking boxes with unrelated contents. We use our minds to graft narratives onto the things we do to our bodies, and the things that are done to them.

The schism between mind and body that is imagined by philosophy and, until relatively recently, by science can be traced back to René Descartes. *I think, therefore I am*, he stated, and with the seventeenth century's understanding of the human organism, he declared the physical structure of the body—limbs, skin, organs, all our warmths and wetnesses—to be separate and divided from that which makes thoughts, emotions, and ideas: the mind.

Neuroscience asks how the contents of our thoughts determine the states of our bodies, and how the states of our bodies determine the contents of our minds. It is perhaps easier to conceptualize the basis for the first question. We understand from our experiences and the common narratives we assign to them that when we are anxious our pulses quicken and our palms sweat. We know the buzzing sensations that arrive as adrenaline floods the bloodstream when we watch frightening movies or experience startle. These links between sensation and emotion are stories we can understand and know how to tell.

But because we can't see or feel the microbiomes of our guts sending information up our vagus nerves to our brains, we tend to hold on to the Cartesian notion of separateness between how we feel and the autonomic bodily processes that are invisible or indiscernible to us. *I think, therefore I am* is an easy truth to swallow, but to also acknowledge that *I*—the I of my gut flora, of my skin movement, of my metabolism, of my hormonal regulation—*am, therefore I think*: that one takes a bit more faith.

When I was working as a dominatrix, I hurt a lot of bodies. Men paid me to hurt them in more ways than I could have imagined. There was much striking—"impact play," in S/M parlance—with objects and with parts of my own body: whipping, flogging, kicking, kneeing, slapping, punching. There was pinching, cutting, slicing, tying. There were medical instruments and hardware store tools and electrical devices that plugged into wall outlets. I sent my clients home with bruises, cuts, abrasions; the impressions of my fingers around their necks in pale purplish pink, vivid striped lash marks on their backs and asses, rope burns around their wrists, ankles, genitals. I knew how to hurt them without leaving a trace, but many of them requested these marks—souvenirs, as it were, of our time together.

I did not, at the time, consider the broader ramifications of the bodily traumas I was inflicting. I considered my work to be self-contained, discrete two- or three-hour chunks of experience in which the effects, like the battering, flowed only outward from my fingers, feet, and fists. Like Descartes, I imagined a split between the acts committed by my body and the contents of my mind, and I did not consider the cumulative effect of these violences, or what might be flowing back into me.

Touch

In fighting, and in training to fight, touch is everything. The narrative of combat sport is built of moments of touch: punching, kicking, kneeing; impact, collision, friction; pull, push, smash. There is gentle touch, too, in muay Thai, the touch of functional care.

Fighters wrap each other's hands, coaches adjust body positions, water is carefully poured into heavy-breathing mouths ringside.

On a date, N and I went to hear a decorated neuroscientist lecture on the sociological importance of touch. I considered how bereft of touch some peoples' lives are—particularly men, for whom the giving and receipt of touch is often a loaded matter. "There is a place for touch in healthcare," the neuroscientist said. There was audible discomfort in the audience's reaction to these words, a collective intake of breath and a low murmuring of protest.

"I know touch can be abused," she demurred in response, though she moved on without elaborating. She delivered a long and engaging talk on the brain–body dialogue, the vagus nerve, the limbic and autonomic nervous systems; high-key science distilled into digestibility for the Tuesday evening crowd.

I wriggled my hand into N's in the dark auditorium and felt the callouses on his palm with my fingers. He rested his other hand on my thigh, and I was immediately a shade more comfortable, full of the warmth and connection conferred by this touch.

When I was a sex worker, more than a few of my clients told me that I was the only person who had touched them in a very long time. They weren't speaking only of sexual touch, but of any human contact. I remember being staggered by the consideration of that fact. A man who doesn't have a partner, whose partner doesn't touch him, or who doesn't receive bodywork like massage might go weeks, months, even years without the touch of another human.

This, of course, can happen to people of any gender, but because of the instability of masculine identity and what Eve Kosofsky Sedgwick termed "homosexual panic"—that is, terror at feeling or being perceived as feeling desire for another man—there is a deep cultural sense, at least in the United States, that touch is not something to be shared between straight men, except in arenas of sport.

Of all the elements of muay Thai fighting, Josh was weakest in the clinch. His long, powerful limbs made him fearsome and confident in the striking moves—punching, kicking, kneeing, elbowing—and his instinct for reading and dodging his opponent's moves protected him from many strikes that would have landed on a different sort of fighter. But he was uncomfortable at ultra-close range and did everything he could to avoid clinch fighting, which is like stand-up grappling, each fighter trying to gain dominance over the other from a range so close they will both step away soaked in the other's sweat, cranking on necks and biceps while trying to leverage grip against angles to make space for knees, elbows, and sweeps.

The clinch is intimate. In N's muay Thai classes, we practiced in pairs. With one of her hands hooked around the back of my neck and the other clamped onto my biceps, my training partner pulled my head down into her shoulder. I could smell her breath, her hair, the salty milk smell of her skin. As we got a few rounds into the hour of drills, I could feel her perspiration through her T-shirt, warm and damp on my forehead. The clinch was the closest contact I had ever been in with another body aside from sex, and the bleeding through of sexuality into this closeness felt impossible to deny or contain. It's not that I was turned on. It was that this much sweaty full-body contact evoked a visceral association with sexuality that was too big, old, and thorough to sever.

In this posture, we took turns at controlling the clinch: first, she pushed me back, two steps, easily bullying me with her larger, taller frame and superior skills. She stepped her lead foot out to the side of my feet, cranked my elbow skyward, and pulled my neck, which was firmly in her grip, down and around. I stumbled and staggered—the intended effect—and she followed with a sideways strike, her knee making contact with my liver zone that was gentle but authoritative: an announcement of where the hurt would have been placed, were we fighting. My head was still pulled down into her shoulder, and dizziness washed in as she moved me again: two steps forward, this time pulling me, and again the sweep, followed this time by a straight knee to my belly.

I felt safer in the clinch than I did on the street. In the clinch, the contact was explicit and honest, and I had consented to it. As a woman in America, my daily life was inundated with incidental unwanted touch, and I was repeatedly stunned by how much anger and pushback often followed my utterances of *Please don't touch me.*

From early girlhood, the social pressure to accept uncomfortable touch in the name of politeness and not making a scene was powerful and pervasive. I don't know a woman who hasn't suffered through an unwanted hug because doing so is easier than saying *No, thank you.* When Kristen Roupenian's short story "Cat

Person," which includes a scene of a young woman having undesired sex with a date because it is easier than extricating herself from his apartment, made the rounds on the internet, I and nearly all my female friends understood exactly how and why one might make that choice. As a younger woman, I made that choice so many times that the incidents are indistinct in my memory.

The older I get, the more I say *Please don't touch me.* I grow less and less comfortable with haphazard touching, particularly from men. I feel embittered toward men as an institution, which can be confusing, because I also love individual men. There is a part of me who is still afraid of being perceived as shrill or uncool; that part tries to find compassion for the truly astonishing parade of men who feel entitled to contact with my body. That part tells me that being touched here and there is not that big a deal. The real truth is that I have become the kind of woman my twenty-year-old self would have rolled her eyes at while paying the tab for her idiot boyfriend. That is to say, I have become a woman who cares to stand up for myself. I want no part of the too-long huggers, the double-hand-handshake grabbers, the upper-arm holders, the lingering cheek kissers. When I receive my change from a purchase, I don't want my palm caressed along with the coins. The emotion that is attached to the cumulative violence of all this unwanted touch is not annoyance. It is rage, hot and blistering. The rage scares me, so I often tamp it down, reminding myself that many of these men were boys who were not taught the boundaries of other people's bodies, that culture has told them they can have anything they grab but they must never show need, that they may have no outlet for healthy touch in their lives. I burn anyway.

I wondered how touch, consent, and violence intersect, and how context and consent alter the effects of violence committed and received, and in seeking answers I returned, full circle, to combat sport. Training to fight is not all violence. There is physical care between men in the practice of martial arts, too. Whether it exists to offset all the roughness exchanged, or whether space is made by these very violences for a culture of touch predicated on tender masculinity, I am not sure, but I do know this: in fighting, embodied conversations take place inside and outside the ring, in which men say things like: *I respect you, I trust you, I care about you, I love you.* They say these things with graciously absorbed blows, with easy embraces before and after sparring sessions, with acts of service undertaken without request or fanfare.

N answered my questions about the masculinity that exists between men who train and fight together, and told me that in this space, the ego and jockeying for dominance that pervade the broader culture was markedly absent. He talked about the humility that came with a daily practice of being physically bested, and how hypermasculinity, with its inherent precarity, had no room to breathe in the ring, on the mat, in the training camp. Because the exploration and expression of dominance was literal and physical in the ring, all the extraneous cultural baggage and identity politics that orbit the idea of what it is to be a man became moot.

Anyone can wax philosophical, and I don't know if I would have bought those claims if not for my own experience of N and the men he trains. N is, by an order of magnitude, both the gentlest and the most dangerous man I have ever known. On the mat

I saw glimpses of what he could do with his body: how lethal his fists, shins, elbows, and knees would be under the right circumstances. We often went running together at night, and next to him I felt free of fear in a way that was new in its completeness; I knew no one would hurt me when he was there. I had known plenty of rough men: men who became unhinged by their anger and perceived powerlessness, men who were careless with their words and hands. N was not this, not anything close to it. He was something else altogether.

I watched the care and tenderness with which he treated the bodies around him. I saw him reach out a hand behind his young son's back as he clambered up a slide, offering just enough support, not quite pushing. I watched him with my friend's small anxious dog, caressing her nervous ears until she nestled in at his feet and turned her belly skyward. I felt him with my own tender parts, which I myself often treated so carelessly, the surfaces of his hands rough with weightlifter callouses but the touch they carried gentle and full of care. My long hair would get pinned under my shoulders when I was lying down in bed, and he would free it without pulling any of it from my head. Even in the boxing studio, where he taught me to punch and threw instructive jabs toward my face, he pulled me close with a gloved hand between rounds and kissed my sweaty forehead.

We can be like puppies together, he told me, about the affection I observed between his team of fighters, *because we understand that we are wolves.*

SKIN HUNGER

I worry, after N and I learn that I am pregnant, that the way we touch each other will change. Specifically, I worry that he will no longer want to touch me in the night and the early morning and the stolen afternoons, that we will lose the minutes and hours in which our limbs stay tangled up in each other and the big goose-down duvet, the sweat beading on my upper lip and his forehead, cooling in my clavicle and navel. I worry that something invisible will shift or recede and we will lose our connection, and that will be it. I try not to hold on too tightly—to him, to anything. But as my world shrinks, I feel myself growing anxious in my attachment, my wants turning to needs in a way that scares me.

During the months of the pandemic quarantine, N is the only person who touches me except for one bodyworker who gives me a masked outdoor massage, one midwife who applies a fetal Doppler to my abdomen, and one technician who doesn't quite touch me but squirts me with warm sticky gel and probes my belly with an ultrasound wand for thirty minutes, counting the limbs and digits and organs of our baby's body, taking inventory of their tiny anatomy. On the inside of my body, our baby pushes against me, and this too is a kind of contact, but it feels as close to touching myself as being touched by another.

I hunger for touch, during this time. I do not receive a hug from my mother, my sister, my best friend. None of them even sees me pregnant, let alone feels my baby moving underneath the skin of my belly, the most wondrous thing my body has ever experienced. I wistfully remember long hugs and casual shoulder squeezes with friends, and the way my friend Lucy would sit down for a long time and comb through my hair with her small fingers, searching, at my request, for gray strands to pull out.

In other ways, though, it is a relief to be fully sequestered from lingering palms and squirmy fingers that I don't want on me. Because my prenatal care has been converted to telehealth video appointments, I haven't had a single vaginal exam during my pregnancy, no searching gloved fingers poking through my unyielding core, no latex pushing into dryness with my head lolling to one side as I try—there is never enough time in these kinds of exams to succeed, but I always try—to disassociate from the slab of meat and bone parts on the table. No one has tried to grope my swollen belly at brunch or in the line at the store, largely because I haven't been out anywhere like that, but also because touch has, in the pandemic, become a topic of focus, an act once often performed without consideration and now incessantly debated on various political shows. Should we still hug, should we shake hands? Should ministers lay hands on their parishioners, should politicians kiss babies? The actual horror of a handshake—transferring every mouth and nose and genital touch each person has absentmindedly engaged in throughout the day, a sweaty acquiescence to the cellular connectivity of our bodies in space—now feels undeniable, and I no longer feel conflicted about refusing one, as for so long I have.

I think a lot about my body: how it feels, what it is doing, what is happening to it. For so much of its existence, this body's purpose has been defined by what other people were doing to it, and that has shifted but hasn't fully changed. On one night or morning or afternoon back in December, while we were catching our breath and falling asleep curled into each other, N's microscopic cells were flooding this body, meeting my cells, and together those cells have grown into a person and occupied it, bastioned by our hope, and now I am not the same. Nearly everything about my physical self has been changed on a chemical level: hormones and proteins and cells, all altered to accommodate our baby. An increase in blood volume, a fast flood of estrogen, a note to my pituitary gland to switch off my menstrual cycle. Elevated basal body temperature, the loosening of joints and ligaments. My hair grows lush and thick. My eyebrows fall out. Something I can't quite pinpoint changes in my face. I don't recognize my smell.

I see now why people call babies their *seed*. It is a gross term, in some ways, but also maybe conceiving a baby is the truest way for one person to say to another, *I have planted myself in you, and you are still soil but not the same soil and you never again will be; you have been implanted.*

I think, too, about hurt and roughness. I am treating my body far more delicately than I am accustomed to. I give it a nap when it feels sleepy, a snack when it feels hungry. I cut reps off a workout if it feels overtaxed. Still, there is a sense that violence is happening deep within, the slow violence of water torture rather than the violence of a car accident. As my body stretches and rends, the ligaments deep in my lower abdomen ache and the joints of my lumbar spine loosen and shift with alarming clicks, pops, and grinding sounds. My skin pulls tight across my belly and my navel closes up. I think about how much violence this body has absorbed, how much hate and desire have been conferred on it by hands that loved using it—love as in *relish*—but did not love me—love as in *care*.

Hidden somewhere in what are now faint white scratches and forever-popped capillaries, residue of knives and hot metal and lit cigarettes and brutal hands, there is still the whisper of visible evidence of how much people have loved using this body. I have tattooed over some of them, let others fade into the background of the stretch marks and skin imperfections that speckle my thirty-seven-year-old skin, but I know where they are, that map of how I tried to find peace in the slice of a belt and the crack of a hard slap.

No one has hurt me in years—not at my request, not through my grimace, not on purpose or by accident or in any way. N's hands are more gentle than I knew men's hands could be. They are not the clammy hesitant paws that pose as gentle to mask discomfort and incompetence—those I know about, those I know grow into something else in dark moments with women who don't have last names: women like I was. That touch—polite touch—I hate more than any other kind, for the untruth embedded in it. N's touch is gentle and honest: firm and sure, never hesitant, his strong palms and fingers closing around mine, holding my neck, grasping my leg, searching me and listening for what he feels.

I thought for a long time that I needed violence to feel anything—to feel attraction, to feel connection or excitement, to come. I thought that being hit was the only way this body could register reaction, because violence was the only thing intense enough to rupture the barrier of my numbness, and maybe at the time I was correct. Or maybe I had just never been touched well. I'm not sure it matters that I know.

BRUTALITIES (II)

After I stopped dominatrixing, I wanted to be done with the feminine arts. Sloughing them off and releasing their privileges was harder than I'd expected, though. Even when I was learning how to weld, and then how to butcher and slaughter animals, it took me a while to quit sex work—longer than I anticipated—and I tried to wean myself off the cash and the intrigue by working very hard at my new, equally ill-suited career welding steel with the union crew on high-rise buildings in Manhattan. I was good at the work, better than anyone expected me to be, but as soon as I graduated from my apprenticeship and started making real money, I fell into the habit of driving four hundred miles every weekend to spend time with Dean at the farm upstate. I would drive straight out of the city after work every Friday, hit traffic on the Harlem River Drive like clockwork, and speed up

I-90 for hours, rolling into the farm long past dark, dirty, lonely, and exhausted. Dean spent most of his time at the farm, going down to the city once or twice a month, and he knew the trek was wearing on me.

You could move up here, you know. With me. We could both live up here.

What about work?

We were sitting on the unfinished deck at the back of the farmhouse, watching the flock of birds mill around the yard. They were on the move, pecking at each other's feet and squawking around the long red-brown slope of the manure pile. We watched them for a while. The rear bumper of Dean's truck was crumpled in and hanging low on the right side.

You could just be here, and not worry about it. Take care of the animals. Or we could do a job together maybe.

I didn't say anything, but after he got up to go fiddle with the truck I got a big colander and took it out to the garden and picked all the cherry tomatoes, a job that I consistently shirked until the fruit would rot on the vine and make slimy little piles of collapsed jelly. We argued about the tomatoes more than once, about the waste. I don't know why I didn't just do it, but I had dug my feet in so much that getting the colander felt like a real offering, squatting out there with wet loam squeezing up between my toes, the air heavy with the sweet tang of the plants, the sun warm on my back. It was lovely in the garden, but it was still and silent, and that has always been difficult for me. I prefer work that is strenuous, repetitive, mindless, and painful, of which there was plenty. I shoveled the endless pig shit out of the stalls in heaping pitchforkfuls without complaint. I jammed the never-sharpened shovel into the rocky ground over and over and over again until it was ready for fenceposts, and then I swung the sledgehammer up and over and around my shoulder again and again until the posts were driven, careful not to miss, that's how you sledge your knee by accident. When the winter loomed Dean paid an Amish man to split us three face cords of firewood from the oak tree that came down in a hurricane, missing the house by just a couple feet. I stacked all three by myself and when I was finished my hands were so swollen Dean had to cut my gloves off for me.

She's my grunt, he liked to say when we were on jobsites together, because I carried everything, all the tools, the material, eighty-pound welders, yards and yards of steel cable. He would lean on the truck and worry a toothpick around the corner of his mouth, blue eyes glinting at me, watching me grunt and lift. *She's got it*, he'd say when anyone tried to help me. He knew I didn't want the help, but that's not why he said it. He wanted to watch me work. He liked having a girl doing all this, though he was neither lazy nor unwilling to do it himself in my absence. He had taught me so much of what I knew about my work, so it felt fair, the interminable apprenticeship wherein I never moved up and he never stepped aside.

Tending the garden was different from working the farm or the jobsite, though. It was slow and tedious and required little physical exertion, so my mind ate at me, same as it did whenever my body was inactive. I avoided most activities that required this sort of half attention, because they made me feel uncomfortable. There was a sense of rush and also of paralysis, of things pent up. A pot left on simmer and walked away from, angry but indolent insects buzzing halfheartedly in a very small space. My relationship with myself was marked by this claustrophobia and unease.

I roasted the tomatoes on a cast-iron skillet. Our stove was a wood burner that Dean had modernized with a propane tank, and the 1920s enamel knobs were loose and imprecise. By the time I opened the belly of the stove to check the skillet, it was so hot that when I flicked water on it the beads didn't even dance around the surface, they just evaporated on contact like they had never existed, like there was a place inside our house where things could disappear altogether. I reached in and grabbed the handle of the skillet with a heavy dish cloth that I had doubled over until it was thick enough to protect my hand. The heat on my arm felt like pinpricks. As I hoisted the skillet out and up to the stovetop, I could feel that I'd done a poor job at folding the cloth, that it was not quite large enough, that the pad of skin on the inside of my thumb was so close to the surface of the cast iron that it was almost touching.

Dean was sitting at the kitchen table, running his finger absentmindedly along the crack in its center. He was talking about installing new fluorescents in the metal shop, about the bid he got from the machinist, about the neighbor up the hill using Roundup. *Maybe we should have the pond water tested, . . . what are we gonna do about the tank of muriatic acid from the aluminum job, it's gonna crack when winter comes and sure it's diluted but that can't be good for the groundwater, . . . the water table.* I didn't know the difference between groundwater and the water table and I couldn't believe he didn't have a plan for the huge plastic cube that we had filled with runoff from the patina for those two-hundred-thousand-dollar trellises we had built.

The tomatoes were black around the edges, wrinkled like toes in the bath, but probably edible. There were spiderwebs inside the soft pleats of the curtains and black soot from the propane all along the underside of the bread warmer and I looked at him and wondered what it would feel like to not have a city to leave to, to not have my own job and my own money and my own truck and an escape hatch for when things got too intense. He was talking about the new woodstove and the assholes at the buildings department who said he needed a permit to install it and fuck them and this was his property and he said it like that, *My property*, not *Ours*, but *Mine*, and for half a second I wondered what that made me, even though I already knew.

Then I pressed my thumb into the cast iron so hard and fast that wet steam rose straight up from it. I felt time grind to a stop. Every thought and question caved. Past and future crumpled like they'd been put through a trash compactor and everything fell into the hot screaming sear of my flesh.

I just can't believe I need a permit on my own goddamn land. He didn't look up, and I didn't make a noise. When I put the skillet down on the range my thumb stuck to it the way chicken skin sticks in a stir-fry pan. The only feeling I could name was hollowness. It was absence, not presence, and the failure to find words was not incidental, it was the intended effect of the whole thing. Inside my forehead there was a rubberiness, something stretching and recoiling, and I suddenly noticed the pulsing of the bare lightbulb dangling out of BX cable over the countertop. Everything else was still.

In the bathroom, I dipped my thumb into a pot of silver sulfadiazine and wrapped it with gauze. I served Dean the burned tomatoes and he ate them, unfazed. For all that could be said about his endless string of demands and dissatisfactions, he always ate my food with gusto. I could feel the beat of my heart in my thumb, pulsing like a bass line. Later, after I awkwardly scrubbed the skillet with one hand, we climbed up the rickety wooden stairs to our summer bedroom. My thumb was still throbbing, and I wanted nothing from him, but when he reached for me I did not pretend to be sleeping, as I sometimes did. I sat straight up on my knees, my toes tucked neatly under me. I pulled off my oversize sweatshirt with the hole in the belly, clasped my hands behind my back, and tilted my face toward him. He slapped me once, hard, and I hardly felt it. I hadn't really been in my body since I started thinking in the tomato patch. He stood and I tipped my face up to him again. It was so dark that I could only see the glinting wetness of his teeth and eyes, but I knew where he was, and he didn't miss. He held my chin in one sandpapery hand, a firm and measured grasp. It was a proprietary touch, the same one he used with the lambs. He slapped me again and suddenly there was light, shiny white like platinum or the surface of the moon, glowing all around me but fading fast the way a dream goes; when I looked for it, it vanished. I felt heat on my cheek, right in time with the sickening crack, but nothing else.

You scare me sometimes, he would say to me later, more than once, in earnest moments, and I know these were the times he was talking about. He smelled sweet and dusty like clover hay, cut through with the spicy animal smell of rough men. I leaned my face into his belly: diesel fuel and line-dried cotton. He put one of his hands on top of my head, smoothed my hair back from my forehead, pulled me in closer.

Are you ok? You seem like you're somewhere else.

For a week I wavered about moving up to the farm. I got dubious advice from a friend who was living with a married man and his wife and pretending to be their nanny. *Do what you would do if you had no fear,* she told me. Bubbling over with Eckhart Tolle–isms and the flush of illicit sex, she flung this jewel at me over lattes in Prospect Park as we sat on benches covered in plasticky green paint pocked with bubbles.

You know what the smart thing to do is, a better friend told me, which is the only kind of advice you can give to someone who won't take any. *Maybe just keep your job,* she said, careful to trail off with the hesitant lilt of a question, though any sane person would know it should have been a statement.

I spent some time thinking about what I would do if I had no fear—fifteen minutes, at least. The truth was that it had been decided long before I went through the routine of considering it.

That October, we bought pigs because we were driving past a place with a sign that said PIGS FOR SALE and Dean had money. We did not know that no one buys pigs in October. People slaughter pigs in October, before the winter comes. During winter, pigs turn into money pits who eat and eat and eat and yet grow thinner by the day, but we did not know this. We also did not understand what it meant to have a drafty crumbling barn in the dead of winter. We had vague ideas about the animals' bodies creating heat and some books about straw bale insulation, but the truth was that we bought the pigs like we bought snacks in the overpriced gourmet bodegas on Bedford Avenue: throw 'em in the bag.

The pigs, as it turned out, were incredibly stressful to tend. We wanted to think of ourselves as good farmers, so we did everything we could for them. We went out to the barn at six in the morning to break open with the blunt wooden handle of an old broom the ice that covered their water, the sweat inside our thermal onesies freezing to a thin glaze of slush next to our skin.

Dean, as it turned out, did not respond to the stress of the pigs very well. I had seen him under stress before, but only the city kind. Job stress, contractor stress, real estate market stress, day trading stress. Poker stress, Certificate of Occupancy stress, Department of Buildings stress, parking ticket stress. *Any problem that can be solved with money isn't a real problem*, he liked to say, and all those stresses were around the accumulation and retention of money. Dean was good at money. The arrogance that hindered him in personal matters was gold for business, and he had enough of it to charge double for what he sold and to lowball what he bought. He got what he demanded, seemingly every time. More than just that, though, he was a great picker. He had an instinct for the untapped resource, the diamond in the rough, the gentrification bubble that hadn't even come out of the wand yet. That eye for the undervalued was accompanied by an uncanny certainty in his ability to do things that he had no experience with. In another era, he would have struck gold in California.

This was why he had plenty of money to make rash purchases of livestock and machinery, always in cash. Since the neighborhood had flipped, the abandoned girdle factory on the wrong side of Brooklyn that he had bought in the early nineties was such a cash cow that he could afford to buy trucks and property in cash. The only problem was that he was also a card player. A good one, which is the worst kind. He slipped away some nights after I was asleep and woke me early in the morning by throwing cash all over me, with the manic glint in his eye that I knew meant he had played well and won. Since the first night I met him, I had never seen him without a roll of bills the size of a small sandwich in his front pocket, bound in half with two or three thick rubber bands. I bought him a money clip once, but he never used it. Not big enough.

I knew he was compensating for something with all the cash, filling the same hole that he filled with the terrible things he said to me on the mornings when he came home after losing. I knew that it was the deep well of pain inside him that made him so arrogant and unkind.

He bought the farm with cash, trying to turn all his money into something else. To spin it into something true and real and invulnerable to influence. So we drove up to the woods where irony didn't live, where a full set of teeth was a pretentious thing to have, and we took responsibility. For him, this was what the animals were for.

Under the lash of a winter colder and longer than either of us had imagined, we took care of the pigs. Four of them, covered in red-brown hair the texture of a Brillo pad. Four of them, cold and hungry and in constant need. They broke the stalls and we fixed them. They injured themselves and we tended them. They ran away and we inched down our icy county road in Dean's big black Dodge Ram, trying to herd them back home in the least effective way possible but the only one we could think of. I worried about their safety and well-being without interruption, while Dean seemed able to turn his attention off when he chose.

While we were out at the grocery store one afternoon, the pigs broke out of their stalls and gained entry to the house. We came home to a scene so comically wretched that I could only sit down on the ground and laugh. The kitchen door was wide open, and every cabinet was splayed open. They had gotten up on the counters, covering everything with the sour porcine stench of their feces and the deeper, softer musk of their body oils. There were hoofprints on the marble, shattered dishes all over the floor, wet smears of pig shit along the baseboards. They ate all the cereal.

When summer came, we brought home two Duroc barrows and a pregnant Hampshire sow. We thought we had become experienced farmers by this point, so we felt ready for a five-hundred-pound animal who cost eight hundred dollars and could need imminent medical intervention at any time. She was so big I was frightened of her, a great heaving mass of flesh rendered in pinks and grays, large enough that I imagined she could kill me just by pressing me between her body and the side of her stall. Her swollen teats all poked in different directions. Her vulva bulged out of her body, an angry pink brighter than anything else in the barnyard.

The farmer we bought her from seemed confident in his prediction of her due date. *Three months, three weeks, and three days*, he told us. Dean and I were both too embarrassed at our urban ignorance to ask the obvious, *From when?* So we brought her home and we plushed her stall up with a double layer of straw and we waited.

June passed and she seemed larger each day. According to our instructions, we kept her in her stall and fed her generously. The waiting felt interminable. She developed sores on the thin skin of her belly, the part where I could see the mottled patches of gray and pink underneath the sparse covering of short hairs. I wanted to clean and dress the sores, but I was afraid that she would bite me. I didn't admit it to Dean, but I was afraid of the pigs, of their needlelike teeth and the reptilian movements of their bodies, of their panicky reactions and frantic irrationality. Afraid of their piercing shrieks, so human in pitch and volume that I thought of a woman being tortured every time I heard them wail.

I am not afraid of stray dogs or unbroken horses. Dogs and horses, no matter how large and fierce, have a logic I can understand. They have instincts I recognize, fears and desires. But the pigs were unpredictable, at times self-defeating in their terror and at others wholly sensible. They were either too smart or too stupid, I'd believe either and I didn't know which. I just knew that every day I filled my five-gallon buckets up with two scoops of wheat, two scoops of corn. I ran lukewarm water that smelled like pipes out of the kinked-up barn hose and I plunged my hand into the bucket almost up to the elbow and I grabbed and stirred until a coarse mash was formed. Every day I did this, yet when I pushed through the door from the feed room to the barn, I didn't know what to expect from the pigs. The farm was full of unpredictable creatures, in the barn and in the farmhouse both, and I learned to approach with caution. Some days they were docile, patiently waiting for me to toss sloppy handfuls into the black rubber troughs at the corners of the stalls, eating with gusto but not aggression. Some days they were already biting each other by the time I got the door open, cutting through thick hide to leave sharp puncture wounds, pushing each other down and stepping on each other's legs, bellies, cheeks to get closer to my buckets. Some days they bashed against the wooden slats that formed the barriers to their stalls, and I heard the thin soggy old barnwood we had repurposed as lumber creak and squeal under the pressure. On those days I imagined what they might do to me if they broke through. Would they just step on me with their soggy cloven hooves until they got to the buckets, or would they turn on me like they turned on each other, carving their teeth into my flesh the same way I do to barbecued ribs?

Once they started eating, they calmed down. The sharp wails faded into contented grumbles, low snorty noises that were half-absorbed into the wet piles of anesthetizing carbohydrates. I liked watching them eat. It was one of the few moments on our farm when I felt competent and useful. I watched their bellies swell as they swallowed without chewing, and I wasn't afraid any longer. It was not them I feared, not exactly. It was their hunger.

July passed and we still did not have piglets. Momma's body was so distended that she could hardly get to her feet. My fear of the morning feeding ritual was lulled into remission by repetition. I was comfortable enough to gently scratch her between the bases of her ears—not while she was eating, but after, when her eyes were half-closed and her face was glazed with visible satisfaction. She seemed to enjoy being touched. Her body had been alone for months. Since she'd been pregnant, she'd been in a single stall, safe from ravenous stags and the rapacious boars, any of which would have eagerly torn her asunder. At our place, the other pigs roamed and rooted around outside, but Momma had to be protected from parasites, from tetanus, from mange. The piglets imprisoned her in her vast ulcerated body, and we imprisoned her in the maternity stall.

On August first she farrowed the litter in the night, with no help from anyone and no need for anything. When I went out to mix the feed in the morning, I found them: twelve tiny piglets, squirming in the straw like minnows, with russet-colored hair and long anteater noses like their daddy, a Duroc. Momma looked like a beach ball with a slow leak. She was on her side and didn't get up when I crashed through the door with the buckets, just lifted her head. She met my eyes. It was the first time I had made eye contact with her.

It feels very natural to look at an animal in the way that I look at a pickup truck or a dinner plate or an earring. The gaze is outward only, and I feel free because I feel unseen. I feel the same way alone, or with a blindfold on my eyes. The feeling is not a consequence of reality, it is a consequence of perception. Once I met Momma's eyes, the place where I thought my looking ended became a mirror. The privacy was gone. She saw me.

The piglets rustled against each other, groping blindly toward her teats, pushing for light and air and food and warmth, experiencing their aliveness in a way that consumed and overwhelmed them. Momma looked into me and I looked into her, and I had no idea what to make of what was flowing between us because she was a pig and I was an emotionally erratic woman who has been to too much therapy and overthinks everything, but what I thought I felt was a communion.

The arrival of the piglets brought back the awareness of how incompetent we were at farming. On their second day of life, Dean headed out to the barn and came running back out ten minutes later, his arms full of a lumpy pink load. When he got closer, I saw that it was three of the babies. Dean was crying the same way he cried when the neighbor's dog killed our ducklings, the way I sometimes caught him doing in the corner of his office, his torso hunched over and a wrinkled photograph of his first dog Nina in his lap.

The first time I saw him cry about Nina I felt jealous. She was magnificent—a Fila Brasileiro, a breed of dog bred to hunt people, one hundred and forty pounds of glossy brindle and muscled jowls. Nina died of a heart attack in Dean's arms, at the top of a hill at the end of a run that was too long on a day that was too hot. He carried her for miles, but her big mastiff heart had stopped beating by the time he got her back to the car, and he was never quite the same afterward.

I wondered, when he told me the story, if he would have done the same for me. If he would have gathered my crumpled weight in his arms and run with me, sweating and stumbling and crying. If that blank spot that he had for me was bigger and colder than his love for me as an animal, a faithful thing, something he had assumed responsibility for.

I knew when I saw him running with the armful of piglets that he was remembering Nina, that his body knew this feeling of having been too powerful and having made a terrible mistake. A life is a heavy weight, something that suspends itself between the brain and the heart and doesn't allow benefit of the doubt.

Two of the piglets were clearly dead, cold and breathless and beginning to stiffen. One was breathing, a harsh and shallow sound tearing out of its gullet. Its belly and loins were covered in a hideous purple-black bruise that looked like a puddle spreading over its most vital and tender organs. *She rolled over on them,* Dean choked out, spittle flying out of his mouth. I took the struggling piglet out of Dean's arms and hurried into the house. He was inconsolable, I knew, and the animal had to come first.

The piglet's eyes were terribly small. This was our first home litter, so I had no idea if this was normal or a consequence of the accident. I tried to look into them, to make contact, to confirm life, but I couldn't. The piglet just stared out with beady intensity, his pain radiating out in the trembling of his body and the low whimpers that came with every few breaths.

I took him into the bedroom and nestled him into the corner of the white velvet Victorian couch that had been fancy before work pants and dog hair and moths and mildew got the best of it. This was where we always took the broken animals. Some of them made it out—the gaggle of goslings whose mother wouldn't let them under her wings, our big beautiful Rottweiler with the wrecked hip, Bigelow the baby goat who couldn't figure out how to latch on to his momma's teat. We heat-lamped and bed-rested and bottle-fed them back to wellness and they left the bedroom and made it back outside, but others weren't so lucky. Our tiny chick who couldn't get her digestive system working: I cleaned her tiny body with a warm wet Q-tip and fed her pinches of presoaked food, but she died anyway. The baby goat with the defective front legs, who never stood up but spent her short life struggling on her knees until her equally defective organs gave out. Our poor duck,

Harold, who lost his leg and then his life to a maggot-eaten infection. We kept those broken babies alive longer than they would have lived without our clumsy interference, and then we allowed our selfish hearts to break when they did the most natural thing any animal can do.

I covered the piglet up with some laundry and gathered the hurt-animal supplies. Plastic bin, straw, baby bottle, heat lamp. It was summertime, and hot, but I knew from a book that shock makes bodies cold in any temperature. I assembled the nest, pushing the straw up high on the sides of the bin so that the piglet's body would be supported. I couldn't yet tell if he was going to die, but each of the animal deaths taught me that what rattles around painfully in my head afterward are the small kindnesses I withheld out of thoughtlessness. I think about how I might feel if I were tiny and terrified and bleeding internally. I think about how I have felt when my body has been broken, when I have feared for my life.

I piled the straw higher, clipped the lamp to the bin, and gently scooped the piglet up from the couch. I meant to put him right in. And yet. There was something about his weight in my arms—not even five pounds, less than a package of sugar—that made me ache deep in my chest. His skin was cool to the touch, and there was a gurgle of foamy spit gathering in the corner of his mouth. The hair on his ears was as fine as a spider's legs and the sun streaming through the dusty windowpanes settled on it, a little sparkly. I was crying by then, cradling the piglet to my aching chest in a motion no one ever showed me but that I felt utterly sure of. My body was made for this, evolved from a time when people were just mammals and the point of everything was to make more people, a time before work boots and checkbooks and Microsoft Word. My soft parts were engineered for a moment just like this, when a helpless wailing thing would need me to quell its fear and sustain its life. It wasn't supposed to be a fucked-up piglet, but there I was.

He didn't make it through the night. When the sun went down for the day the summer heat receded with it, so it took a while before I noticed how cold and still the piglet's body was. I put my ear to the side of his belly, hoping to hear the light fluttering thump of a tiny heart, but there was nothing. His legs were beginning to stiffen, and I suddenly understood I had played a trick on myself with hope and guilt and impotence, that I had been holding on to a dead thing for some hours.

In the morning I drove down to the city, still wearing my sour-smelling barn clothes, my hands stained with the milky smell of the piglet and my hair studded with straw. *I'll take care of it*, Dean said when I asked him where we should bury the body. We had eaten pork shoulder and loins and homemade bacon every day for the past week. If the piglet had lived we would have let him grow broad and round and we would have killed and eaten him too. It was baffling, where I drew the lines in my head, with my heart, where I doled out compassion and respect and where I claimed my privilege to possess and destroy. When the animals died prematurely—and by this I mean before we chose to take their lives—we felt great cavernous sadness in our chests, both of us. We ached with feeling and remorse and compassion and regret. We could have done more, been better, worked harder, known more. We could have husbanded these animals more competently, the better to usher them toward the deaths that we had pre-decided not to feel upset about.

When they died by accident we buried them with a piece of fruit. We had an odd somber ritual we hardly discussed. I can't remember its origin. Dean dug the hole. I wrapped the cold stiff bundle in a dish cloth or a feed bag or whatever scrap of fabric I could find. I placed the package in the ground, Dean nestled the fruit on top and then covered them with soft shovelfuls of loamy upstate earth, studded with rocks and worms and shiny snails. He patted the ground level with the backside of the shovel and sometimes we said a prayer, which is an odd thing for two people without religion to do. It was a performance of some kind, or maybe just a stab in the dark, an imitation of what we imagined different kinds of people would do in the face of death. I was comforted by the existence of a ritual around our grimmer mistakes. That we might believe in something, even if it was just ourselves, felt important.

I put a ripe peach on the edge of the kitchen table on my way out the door. *To send with him*, I told Dean, though he already knew what it was for. I drove away, half wishing I had stayed for the burial, half grateful I didn't have to, and by the time I put fifty miles between me and the farm, I had almost convinced myself I'd never felt anything at all.

I left the farm in autumn, five years after I first arrived, two years after our first litter of piglets. By the time I left, everything was dead or gone. After all the animals, it was an odd feeling, to be responsible for nothing. It felt like weightlessness, as if an anchor I hadn't been aware of had been loosened in the night and I could float away somewhere and nothing would be altered by my absence.

I didn't want to leave. It wasn't my plan. My plan was to get in the Westfalia camper van Dean and I had packed to the gills, which had a bad clutch and could only be started by pushing from the back, running alongside as it picked up speed, and then jumping in the flapping door before the van got going too fast. It was full of art books and power tools and tins of smoked fish. The heater barely worked, so we planned to drive straight south, through Virginia and the Carolinas, then to veer west when the temperature got high enough for the wipers to stay unfrozen. We made the plans together, to head to Texas for Dean to find the echo of Donald Judd and wait out the winter, then to LA, where my writing class would start in March. I didn't have much money left after spending the year upstate, but Dean's Brooklyn tenants sent him thousands in rent every month, and we had been living as a team for a while by then. He collected the checks, I did the bookkeeping. I had quit my job. It had not occurred to me to worry about my dwindling bank balance, or about my long-term employment prospects as second-chair vagabond living in a van. I trusted him completely.

In Texas he would make sculptures. It was only when he was making sculptures that he was happy, and it was only when he was happy that he was kind. So in Texas, he would be kind. I was only happy when he was happy, so in Texas, I would also be happy. I had never been to Texas before, and a van, no matter how twee and German, is close quarters for two people who sometimes fail violently to get along. But I had hardly considered these factors, because I had decided that in Texas we would be happy. It was just a matter of getting there.

To have a farm is to be rooted to one place, beholden to feeding schedules and broken fence lines and deworming protocols. Animals are inherently stabilizing to the people who tend them, because their needs are regular and predictable and relentless. I often felt suffocated by these demands, by the early mornings and the long drives to the grain supply, by not being able to go away for a weekend or spend money recklessly without considering what it would mean for the animals. But I felt this imposition like discipline, and while I did not always receive this discipline comfortably, I mostly understood that it was molding and shaping me into something better. Dean was different. Wilder, more defiant, one of those horses that would break its own legs trying to escape before submitting to a halter. He bucked the schedules, the demands, the common sense. He asked why when it was not relevant or helpful, and he insisted on iconoclasm when conformity would have better served.

When we began talking about leaving for the winter, I had a long list of reasons why not. The animals, for one. And money. And our house, still half-dressed in gray-stained Tyvek that whipped in the wind like a long billowing skirt.

But we can't leave. The pipes will freeze. The roof could leak. The silo might collapse. With each of these protestations, I saw his eyelids clench closer and closer into a furious squint until he was glaring at me like a big jungle cat. In the wild, it is important for prey animals always to be attuned to the fine movements of predators.

I will not, he over-enunciated—another sign that I had

overreached—*stay here all winter with you just because you are afraid. I will not*—here the *T* sliced through the air like a knife sliding against a sharpening stone—*be told what to do by you.*

I could sometimes see it coming in the arch of his eyebrows, a certain imperiousness that descended as if from an off-site cloud of fury, ready to be weaponized into rage with a few moments' notice. But by the time his voice switched from easy New York fast talk to the clipped diction of a drill instructor, I had already missed too many signals.

Your fear is disgusting, he began. *I don't want it around me, it's toxic. You would try to make rules for me in my fucking house?* I could feel his engine turn over and slide into gear as his rage started, first low in his belly, then spilling out of his chest.

So we decided to pack the van and head south. We decided this by way of him saying *I hate you*, and me saying *But I love you*, and him saying *I don't want you to come with me*, and me saying *But I will be perfect.* We decided this by him driving fast out the driveway without letting his engine warm up and me sitting with my bare skin on the splintery wood of the porch, wrapped in a blanket that smelled like musty cedar and spilled tea and the body odor of our dead dog. I sat until the sun went down, feeling inconsolable, and when the cold crept too far into my face and my feet I moped back into the house, where I curled up on the creaky bed in one of the back bedrooms and mercifully slept the rest of the day away.

When he came back I could tell he had been to the casino and won. I don't know how I could tell, it is a certain paying of attention that was cultivated so early in my life that I can't see the mechanisms of it. At six years old I could tell whether my father was warm and jovial or icily brooding, just from how our apartment door sounded when he walked through it. I'm a watcher, and a listener, but it's more than that, it's another sense, a vigilance to emotional frequency that is trained always on men.

By the time Dean was standing next to the bed, I was fully alert. I could smell him, diesel and wool and cold air. The moonlight illuminated his silhouette.

Get up, he growled, and reached into my scalp for a rough handful of knotty hair. Living in the country gave me permission to quit all the beauty rituals that are required of women in the city, and no more blowouts and facials and pedicures quickly degenerated into no more hair brushing or face washing or changing out of work clothes. I looked like a messy little country girl and presented as so young in my sneakers and baseball hats that I was sometimes mistaken for Dean's daughter.

I hate having my hair pulled. I always have, since my over-committed mother used to rip a fine-tooth comb through my snarls with one hand while packing school lunches with the other. Unlike some other kinds of pain, it makes me angry. He hoisted me out of the bed by my head, holding it high while I scrambled to arrange my limbs under it. I swallowed the anger into a hot roiling bolus that settled in my low belly. Everything was happening very slowly. He led me down the long windowless hallway toward the kitchen. Safe in the darkness, I let my face break into a wide smile I knew better than to reveal. This would be ugly, I knew, but it didn't matter. At the end of it I would have my power back.

The next day, with a few tender bald spots on my head, I began to pack the van. After I filled the storage areas with clothes, linens, power tools, and nonperishable food, I cleaned the farmhouse, sweeping a few long snarls of brown hair into the heavy metal dustpan along with coffee bean crumbs and mouse droppings. The inside of my cheek was purplish black, and Dean hadn't spent much time in the house, but everything was settled. We were going to Texas together.

For us to leave, the animals had to be dealt with. The van couldn't handle the highways with any serious snowfall, so we had to leave before Thanksgiving. The days were ticking by quickly, and Dean was gone, collecting money and looking in on jobs and wrapping up loose ends in the city. We were leaving in ten days or a couple weeks. I was too overwhelmed to check the date.

There was a lot of killing yet to be done. We placed most of the animals somewhere—our two horses at a boarding farm, our birds given to Milo, the Amish man who chopped our wood. Milo didn't exactly want the birds, but when we showed up on his land with a truck full of squawking cardboard boxes, he gave us a long slow nod and sliced the packing tape open with his knife. Our chickens, who could fly just enough to make them flighty but not enough to actually take flight, pushed their way out of the box, jumped off the edge of the tailgate, and toddled hopefully toward Milo's dark sweet-smelling barn. Our tom turkey, beloved to Dean, looked befuddled and followed the flock, dodging the hot stream of diesel fumes pushing out of the back end of the truck. The geese went last, and we were not sad to see them spread their wings and screech their unveiled threats to the rest of Milo's animals as they crested their elegant necks and reached their beaks to the sky. They were violent animals, the geese, lacking both the fear and the sweetness of the other birds, their sleek profiles belying the unpredictable meanness of their nature. I was dive-bombed by them more than once, as was Dean. We knew their beaks left mean welts. To catch them, we had to use bath towels and feed buckets, sprinting around our back field in pursuit for a long afternoon. Milo gave us another inscrutable nod as Dean pressed a thin fold of cash into his hand for feed.

Y'all have a good winter, he told us, the crinkling skin under his eyes the only evidence of his smile, which was otherwise hidden under his voluminous red beard. Milo has never driven a car, but he once took a train to Arizona with all eight of his children in tow to seek medical treatment for his mother-in-law. He told me this in my truck one day as I was driving him home after we hired him for a day's labor, as is expected of any English who do business with the Amish. His farm was forty minutes from ours, and I loved those drives. I loved his unfamiliar smells and Pennsylvania Dutch accent, how he was my age but felt wizened like a grandfather. I thought, when he told me about seeing the Appalachian Mountains and the Sonoran Desert out the window of the train, that maybe there was a wish in there, a wistful thought about unchosen options. The world was right there, passing before him every day with hybrid vehicles and microwave popcorn and drive-through cappuccinos. He once asked me for a photograph, which is expressly forbidden by his religion, of a neighbor's Christmas light display. *I just want to look at it later,* he explained, shrugging his shoulders, and I wondered what else this gentle man who worked from dawn to dusk in calm indifference to everything I am in thrall to might want.

Dean also loved Milo. He was something of a spiritual figure to us, which is not at all fair to put on a man who is only trying to muddle through life a little differently than the rest of us, but we couldn't help it. His gentleness and lack of appetites struck us dumb, and we tried not to ogle, but our fascination crept out in our questions, our confusions, our long looks. Not all the Amish men were like this. Some were sloppy and angry and covetous, just like any men. But Milo was different, and it was visible in everything from the way he sat on a bucket in the corner to eat his sandwich at lunchtime, neither consumed with his own thoughts nor engaging in conversation, looking at nothing, just being there, a man on a bucket eating a sandwich, gentle even to the space he occupied.

He called me on my cell phone a few times a year, just to check in, using an English neighbor's phone that all the local Amish made use of. The neighbor would take messages and walk them up the road. We talked about the weather and the stars, which he could read. In another life maybe he would have been a navigator.

When Dean left and I was alone with the pigs, I called the neighbor's phone and asked to leave a message for Milo.

You want I should tell him to catch a ride? she asked. *I think his cousin's working around your way.* I said yes and spent the night shivering between two heating pads, watching television on my laptop while moths clogged up the screen. I was afraid of what had to happen, and when I am afraid, I retreat.

Have you taken care of the pigs yet? Dean asked me on the phone the next day.

Not yet, I replied.

What have you been doing, then?

Packing and cleaning. I covered the beds with plastic sheets and boxed up all our clothes. Cleaned the kitchen out. Got the vacuum seal bags ready.

You know they have to hang for a while, right? We're gonna run out of time if you don't do it soon.

I know.

His voice was half-impatient and half-gentle. All I had to say was that I was afraid, that I wasn't sure I could do a good job, that I couldn't do it by myself. He understood those things, especially when it came to the animals, because he felt all of them too. But I was afraid that what would follow would be, *Why don't you just stay for the winter?* Or *Maybe it's too much for you to take care of in time.* Or, worst, *I'm going to leave without you.* And there was nothing that I wouldn't do to avoid that. It was a gross and unwieldy truth, but I stared it in the eyes too many times to pretend I didn't know its depths. There was nothing I wouldn't have given up to keep him, no part of myself I wouldn't conceal or compromise or serve up like meat on a platter.

And so I knew I had to kill our recent litter of piglets. I had to do it right then and I had to do it myself and it didn't matter that they were young, younger than anyone kills piglets, or that since we wrenched their momma out of the stall a few weeks ago they had been clustered around each other like they had a preternatural idea that someone was coming for them next. In those end times I had to play god and executioner whether I liked it or not, because the alternative—to admit my incompetence and insecurity, to confess that it did something to my heart to slide a blade into soft unsuspecting flesh—carried with it more consequences than I could bear, and if I was anything I was selfish, following my disoriented heart down a questionable path to a dark and ugly place.

The next day, like magic, Milo arrived at the end of our driveway. I had done all the packing and cleaning I could possibly do and the only chore left was to process the piglets. The sheep were stacked in vacuum-sealed cuts in the freezer, their heads and hooves buried in a big rotting pile of blood and bones by the edge of the property line. They were easier, because they were full grown, because Dean and I had done them together, and because unlike pigs, ruminants are deeply trusting and never seem to know that you are about to cut their throats. They went quietly—peacefully, I told myself—sitting on their haunches while we hugged their bodies tight and sturdy. They didn't cry and they didn't flail and they could be easily coaxed with a small tin of grain.

Pigs know, though. Many people believe they are smarter than dogs. They always know.

Milo took care of the piglets for me and never once acknowledged the unspeakable selfishness of prematurely ending their lives so that I could go on a road trip. He did it in the barn and every hour or so walked over to the house with a tarpaulin armful of quartered carcasses. It was so cold in the butchering room that I was afraid I would slice my own flesh and not feel it. My apron was covered with crystallized frozen blood and fat, and my hands prickled with impending frostbite.

When it was all done, I drove Milo home. He cleaned his knife in the driveway before getting into my truck. We hardly spoke on the drive, and when I dropped him off at his own farm, the coil of smoke rising from the chimney and the warm hearth smell from his woodstove made me feel achy and wrong, so alien from the idea of a huge warm family that churns butter together and takes turns getting up to stoke the fire that I didn't even get out of the truck; I just handed him a wad of cash, which he accepted without counting, tucking it into the breast pocket of his work shirt. I thanked him weakly and drove through the dusk, over underboughs littering the county road, past barns that had crumbled in on themselves and trailers sagging at awkward angles, past wavy glass windowpanes spilling over with cheery yellow light, past rusted tractors and parted-out trucks. In the debris of this land I wanted to see some kind of poetic hopelessness, or hopefulness, or anything really, that would allow me to graft a narrative onto the sore swelling feeling in my gut.

When I pulled back into the driveway and killed my engine, the farm was quieter than it had ever been. I was the only living creature on the land, except maybe the mice in the barn. The piglets were dead. Their stalls smelled like wet straw and iron and the freezer was so full of petite plastic packages that the lid wouldn't fully close.

Dean came back a few days later, to collect me and the van and assess my work closing up the farm. I had covered with plastic everything that could be eaten by mice and moths, had thrown out everything perishable, and had disconnected all the appliances except the chest freezers. When the pained whirring of the

jerry-rigged antique icebox had shuddered to a silence, the quiet-
ness that descended was heavy and laden with guilt and fear. I
thought I could hear my own heart beating.

He came back rushed and angry after too many nights at the
underground poker houses and not enough sleep and frustrations
with the tenants. I was angrier than I understood, resentful of the
flashing images of tiny hooves and snouts, tails still covered with
the downy fluff of a baby animal. I hadn't wanted to go to Texas
and I hadn't wanted to kill the piglets and I hadn't wanted to end
up cold and bloody and afraid of being left alone. I had signed up
for a bucolic gingham-apron fantasy, not a horror movie of back-
woods dysfunction, and I was mad about it.

So when he suggested that I should have boxed our clothes up
differently, that I should have put more of the art books in the van,
that I should reconnect the icebox and defrost it again in a few
days, that I had filled the van with too many of my own belongings, a tiny rip opened in my carefully maintained mantle of
patience and devotion. I felt it happen, a ruined stitch over a critical seam tearing open into a gaping hole of fury as words spilled
out of my mouth, all starting with *You didn't* and *You haven't* and
You couldn't, until I reached a crescendo and was crying so furiously that I could no longer talk.

He sat at the bare kitchen table as I bellowed, drinking tea out
of a Mason jar, staring at me like I was a flailing animal on which
he didn't want to waste energy wrestling to the ground. This was
a critical reversal of roles, me furious and him calm. My anger
picked up so much steam that I was no longer conscious of consequence, and as I threw off the heavy yoke of my caution I felt
absolutely intoxicated by my rage. His eyes were glowing ice-blue,

and had I noticed that I would have been alarmed, but my own eyes were stinging and squinting with bright blinding wrathful tears. I was screaming for every time my neck wanted a soft touch and got the prints of five fingers, every time I wanted to be folded into an embrace and got a slammed door and squealing wheels, every time I needed to be told I was loved or valuable or smart or beautiful and instead was stained with the worst, most violent words the language contains. I needed to cleanse myself of all this resentment before I got into the van, before the world shrank again. Every time I followed him the quarters got smaller and the relationship muscled itself into greater and greater magnitude in relation. The farm was small enough, these ten acres of bruises and harshness, of spilled blood and unheard screams. On the farm, there was pain, yes, but also there was space. I held myself together in my secret hayloft hiding spot, the deep woods behind the land, my truck, the bathroom. But in the van? In the van there wouldn't be anything but pain.

The van, with its manual German transmission that I could not operate, with one key that I did not possess, with all my options and agency streaming out the windows as we would head south to a place where I would have no money of my own and no people to call. What a fucking nightmare. Even in the midst of my fit I knew the van was a terrible place for me, and I screamed all the louder for knowing so and not being able to voice it. Even in my loss of control, I still did hold back.

He let me go on for longer than I expected. I don't know that I would have stopped without him stopping me. My voice was hoarse and my cheeks were sore by the time he stood up and pushed the table so hard two of its thick wooden legs left the ground.

Shut up, he bellowed, his starting volume so much louder than the apex of my outburst that I was immediately shaken into silence.

Shut up, again, though I was no longer making any noise. He smashed the Mason jar on the ground and I watched the cold wet tea spread across the flaking barn-red paint on the floorboards until it reached my feet. The slowing of time felt elastic, like I was watching taffy being pulled in slow-motion reverse. He was yelling and I couldn't tell what he was saying until he settled on a familiar refrain: *Stupid, stupid, stupid*, with pain and anger and disbelief. *Stupid, stupid, stupid*, with fury and frustration and sadness.

I waited for him to move toward me, my stomach clenched in certain anticipation. We had been doing this dance for long enough that we both knew the moves by heart. But he didn't, and his volume dropped, though he didn't stop muttering *stupid, stupid, stupid* and shaking his head and looking at me. He was crying too, which was not part of how this was supposed to go. He was supposed to choke me and scream at me and then fuck me and slap me in the face and I was supposed to cry again at the outrage of it all. I was supposed to make a large and luxurious breakfast and apologize profusely while he steeled his jaw and said *I just don't know*, and I was supposed to beg him not to leave me and to promise to be better. That was the dance.

But he didn't reach for my neck. He stepped over the shattered Mason jar, the glass crunching under his boots like brittle bones, and he run-walked out the door, up the hill to the metal shop, where he slammed the door and turned one small light on and appeared to stay there all night, at least until I fell asleep watching the shop from the window.

In the morning I woke up with a crick in my neck and a nervous weight in my gut, like I had been filled with something toxic. His truck was neatly parallel parked next to the metal shop. The van was gone. I called him and left a message. I apologized for my behavior and promised to be different and asked what kind of pancakes he would like for breakfast. He could be at the casino. He probably went to the casino. Or maybe he went to run an errand, some last-minute pre–road trip vehicle repair, some unpaid account, it could have been anything, really. We were leaving the next day and he always left things like paying the insurance and filling his prescriptions and buying clothes to the very last minute. Surely he was doing something like that.

I couldn't get him on the phone but the cell service was always spotty upstate so probably he was on his way back, driving around the lake, the van's tires slippy on the slick stretch of road behind Glimmerglass, his focus on driving. I pulled a bag of bananas, a bag of blueberries, a stick of butter, and a sack of almond flour out of the freezer. I had cleaned the house of most of the food, but it was important that I make homemade breakfast after we fought like this, because it was the only way I could begin to win him back. The bananas were frozen too solid to mash, and I held them in my hands to soften them until I could squeeze them into a slimy pulp.

I knew something was wrong. But I had trained the muscle that ignores intuition and evidence so well that I just pushed that knowledge elsewhere as if it didn't exist. The part of me that is animal and wanted to stay alive had been silenced and suppressed for so long that I could hardly hear it, it was barely a whisper at the end of a long drafty hallway. But still, I knew. I always knew.

I made the pancakes and they went cold on the marble countertop and I disconnected the propane tank and I threw the pancakes
away and I called and called and called and called. The roiling
knot in my low belly was growing in size and strength and I could
not feel any other part of my body. I tested the pad of my thumb
on a razor knife to verify this, and I was correct.

Hours later he picked up the phone, after I had called so many
times the voicemail box was full. I was hysterical by the time I
heard his voice, the voice I always feared and always loved and
always listened to.

I'm not coming back, he said, and for a few seconds I understood and then something happened to me that felt like prickly
ice on my lower forehead and burning on my ears and like gravity had been suspended in favor of intense tremors both within
and without. I dropped the phone. I picked it back up. My hands
weren't working correctly so I jammed it between my ear and
my shoulder.

What do you mean? I asked him, and he said *You know it has to
be this way* and then all I could say was *No, no, no, no no no no no,*
more forcefully than I had ever said it or anything else in my life,
more afraid than I ever had been.

He used to leave a lot. He had been leaving for years, a decade
maybe, so there was a thin stab of hope that felt like the shock of a
too-bright stripe of cold noon sun through a timidly opened window blind. But there was something that felt different, this time. I
went outside to the pond until I was too cold to feel my limbs, and
then I climbed up the ladder to our sleeping loft and stayed there
for a long time, until the sun faded and the stab of hope slipped
away along with it. My body felt dull and heavy, like I was swad-

dled in choking fabric. I curled up small and felt all the minuscule debris in the bed, tiny shards of pebbles, wisps of spiderweb, food crumbs, the onionskin wings of dead bugs. I felt everything on my skin, through my damp clothes and the sheet and the lumpy down comforter, as if I had been granted some incredibly mundane form of extrasensory perception.

For the first time, I did not know which way to go. What was happening in my mind felt terrifying, a great wrenching, breaking, and splitting that I had no words for, coming from someplace so close I couldn't get free of it but so far away I couldn't locate it. I had always known what to do with confusion, despair, and agony. I had methods, ways of dissolving them so they could leak out of me and evaporate away. I had sliced, burned, and splayed myself open for arbitrary horrors that granted me something preferable to the swirling madness in my mind. I had bled and gasped and begged and gagged, and by doing so I had retained the ability to turn off the faucet in my mind, to know myself as a bundle of meat and bones and dampness rather than the vessel for a thing more painful than any of that, a thing I felt I might die before submitting to.

For a long time I'd harbored the suspicion that a time would come when my ways wouldn't work any longer. When I would find myself chest to chest with a feeling too great and too hungry to remain unaltered by its breadth and heft. I thought of this in an abstract way and I saw it in the terrified eyes of the animals and I thought if I could just go deep enough into the recesses of my body, maybe I would be able to dodge it for my whole life, but there I was, with a two-dimensional slideshow of my various tricks and tactics dully flipping in my mind, and I understood, with the blunt force of more apathy than I had ever felt before, that the only ways out from under this pain were to sit through it or to destroy my body forever.

In a house where people hurt each other for recreation, certain objects take on unexpected meaning. In the farmhouse, a coiled belt, for example, could never not make me think of a broad hot sting on my flesh. A pile of rope always made me think of raw scratchy burning around my throat. A blade was a cold feeling just above the clavicle, and a plastic clothes hanger could not be separated from the sharp sound of its angles sizzling through the air and cracking over my backside. The question of how much damage my body could tolerate had been the open question of the last decade, and alone with these objects, the question pushed at me again, loud.

The dead piglets were in deep freeze by then, the white moss of freezer burn creeping around their bagged-up parts. I thought of razor blades and ceiling joists and the sharp turn over the gorge on Skaneateles Road. I thought of the way my breath caught in my throat when Momma and I first met eyes, and of the sound I had heard when Milo went back to the barn for the last time, the final shriek from the last of the small brothers just before he took them with his knife. Animals fight for their lives.

The house was getting colder. I hadn't lit the woodstove all day, and the toilet water was frozen into a shimmering sheet of ice. I didn't know what to do with myself, in a practical sense—where to go, who to call, any of it. I sat and shivered and curled up and lay down, waiting for the acute phase of whatever was happening to me to pass.

And it did. In two days I was so numb I couldn't feel anything at all. My lips were so cold that when I finally made a telephone call to arrange a rental car, they didn't work properly. By then, all the terrible feelings were somewhere on the other side of the room, hanging over my shoulder like a storm slowly rolling out. They never quite left my rearview, but they hung back, a greater mercy than I had dared to hope for.

He never came back.

I saw him two more times, for less than twenty minutes each time. There were things to wrap up: accounts and passwords and login information, titles and deeds and Polaroid photographs. I left almost everything behind in the farmhouse. My truck, my clothes, my Bolivian stone mortar and pestle, the four-hundred-pound butcher block I had wrestled out of an old meat processing plant in Utica with three men I paid to help me. Our dog Max's ashes in the coffin-shaped wooden box, my tools, my special plates, my dignity, my heart. I left with my body and a rental car and a cigarette-burned jacket and two backpacks of books. I left without knowing where I was going.

After we exchanged and disbanded everything we had put together, I never saw him again. I didn't want to see him. I was afraid to see him. But he was still close to me for a long time, because I saw him every day in the fingerprints he had left on my body. I saw him in the scars, some long, sharp and geometric, some jagged and sloppy, and I felt him, the way he had trained me to feel. Every time I ran so long and hard that I threw up and kept going, I felt him, and every time I found a hard hand to strike my face, I felt him.

After a year, I paid a woman to cover the place where his name was tattooed on my arm. She covered it with a tattoo of a peacock feather. I can see, through the eye of the feather, the echo of where his name was, but no one else can.

CAN I SHELTER YOU?

TUCSON, JUNE 2020, 108°

QUARANTINE WEEK 13, GESTATIONAL WEEK 30

As N flies home from coaching a UFC fight, the world falls apart again, anew. Another Black American has been brutally murdered by a cop, and this most recent instance in the never-ending series of similar murders at the hands of the police is filmed. Everyone with internet or television and the will to watch it sees George Floyd beg and struggle on the ground and ultimately die in nine agonizing minutes with a white cop's knee pressed against his neck. Protests have broken out across the country, and police have already turned violent, rushing in with military tanks and semi-automatic rifles, with dogs and tear gas. Protesters are losing consciousness, eyeballs, their lives.

I pick N up from the airport and we get two whole chickens from the drive-through Mexican chicken place. He reads on his phone that Arizona has set an eight P.M. curfew, that the National Guard has been mobilized. We flop on the couch and eat too much chicken. I want chocolate or something else sweet but it is already eight thirty, and even though the terms of the curfew allow for food shopping, it seems too frivolous to send N out into the uncertain world for something so nonessential. We watch horrific footage on the internet as we eat, of people's bodies being shot and gassed and punched and dragged and knelt upon by police. I don't want to watch any of it, but it feels like the very least I can do, to watch the truth in all its ugliness as it unfolds. I am surprised by none of it. I remember with crisp clarity walking with my grandmother near Seventh Avenue in Manhattan on the day the Rodney King riots began, remember her rushing me, and my parents feeling tense and my not understanding what was going on or why the route we usually took home had suddenly become a dangerous place, what that kind of danger even meant.

It is impossible to understand the functioning of the combination of this violence, the utterly apathetic response by the systems of law and order, the months of quarantine, and the new sense of existential precarity brought on by the pandemic and the lockdown and the economic collapse of the country and much of the world. In this context, the unrelatedness of the violence of the streets and the violence of the UFC cages feels clearer than it ever has. In the cage, everyone has agreed to be there. No one is fighting under duress. In the streets, neither of those things is true.

When we finish eating N immediately falls asleep curled up on the couch, his body warm next to me. I look at his softly closed eyes, so sweetly beautiful, and think about what our baby will look like. I feel them kicking and moving around inside me. The gas line at the new house hasn't been turned on yet so we don't have laundry or a stove or hot showers, but I don't care about any of it, I will sit here and eat cold chicken and take a cold shower and wear a dirty shirt with a true smile on my face, scared of the world but cozy in our house, mentally frayed and yet safer than I've ever been.

I was lucky, so fucking lucky, to grow up under circumstances wherein my body was not in peril. All the peril it landed in was later, and much of it was my own doing, and while I have known the cold terror of bodily vulnerability exploited, I have not lived a life marked by such episodes. For me, they were that: episodes. Not the backdrop of my reality. My dalliances with powerlessness were all, to varying degrees, facilitated by the privilege that I had and have. To toy with danger is only a game to people with the opportunity to stop playing, and I am protected by my whiteness and the privilege of having grown up with my father's money with every breath that I have ever taken.

Our baby moves around my belly as I start to doze, full of chicken and glazed over by television and the comfort of N's presence. I think about who our baby will be, and I wonder how the world will flex and yield for them, if they will feel the same safeties and dangers I have or the ones N has or some other set altogether. I wonder what it will mean to be mixed-race in 2025, 2030, 2040, and on. I think about N.'s lost surname, the one his Japanese family changed to keep themselves safe in a racist America, which we will give to our baby next to N's European family name. I think about the first name our baby will receive from N's Hawaiian family, the one most people outside of Hawai'i will struggle to pronounce.

What will I tell our child about violence—the violence of the United States, of the world, of Tucson, of my own life? How will I accept that there will likely be an aspect of my mixed-race child's life that I, a white parent, will never fully understand, that I will only be able to observe? How will I explain the ways women are afraid, the ways men are dangerous, the treacherous ways whiteness is deployed? Will I try to create a cocoon for them with homeschool and no television and lies of omission, in which I pretend it is possible to live in perpetual ignorance of pain and damage? Or will I be brave and honest and tell them whole truths, the ugly parts about myself and this country and this world? I don't know how much truth you're meant to hand to a child. Shelter is safety, but also it can be harm. What will I tell them when they draw their small finger across the scars on my body and ask what they are, just as I remember doing with my own mother's body? What will I tell them if they, as I have, seek things that hurt them? Will I act as if I am a person without a complicated history of violence and suffering, or will I allow them to see me as I actually am, tatters and triumphs knit together? What will I tell them about my life and its pains, about the truths I have learned, about the things I have written?

On the video footage a young Black woman, masked for both anonymity and protection from Covid, speaks to a reporter. The reporter asks the protester somewhat obtuse questions about what she wants and why she is out demonstrating, and I hear both the quaver and the power in the protester's voice, her fear and her desperation and also her bravery and her love. Her body is slim and small. I shudder to think of her at the hands of one of the beefy cops patrolling all the areas of our country—hers and mine— with military-grade weapons and zero accountability. Over her mask, her eyes flash anger and fear and adrenaline. Smoke, or maybe gas, filters through the air behind her. I can hear sirens and gunshots and explosions on the shaky audio. My body is calm and warm and fed and safe. My baby, insulated from all this violence by the layers of my own body, shifts peacefully, wriggling to find a more comfortable position. The reporter asks the young woman her name and she stiffens at the question. *You can call me Jane Doe*, she says, looking around behind her in a way I can tell she has been doing since she was very young. *Stay safe, Jane*, the reporter says. My baby settles. I turn the phone off. N wakes up and we walk down the long Saltillo-tiled hallway and climb into bed and reach for each other, our bodies familiar comforts, our bodies known and safe. Outside, there is chaos in downtown Tucson. We are safe inside, our baby safe inside me. The guilt of my relief at our safety lives in my chest, near my solar plexus. His body smells like water and sun. His skin touches mine and I can't tell any longer where he ends and I begin. We fall asleep curled into each other, my breath shallow, his warm heavy arm wrapped around me, the ceiling fan whizzing, the taste of each other in our mouths, and rest like we were tranquilized.

IN THE CLINCH (II)

Weight

The evening before Josh's fight, I met N at a sports bar in downtown Tucson to watch the fighters weigh in. The place was full of fighting people, easy to spot by their builds and the sets of their jaws. I arrived early and spent a few minutes scanning the room, watching bodies move around the space. There was a medical scale and a microphone set up in the corner, along with the promoter's flag, which the fighters would pose shirtless in front of after being weighed. No one was drinking anything, and I guzzled my club soda guiltily, knowing some of the fighters had spent the past twenty-four hours sweating every possible ounce of water out of their bodies so they could make weight. It was obvious who was there to be weighed in: they looked skinny, hungry, vulnerable. In the training camps, the fighters had been manipulating their bodies, their appetites, and their survival instincts for months now, and each carried palpable residue of those efforts in their posture and mien. They were parched and starving, their faces cavernous and wan. The combination of visible musculature and visible starvation was an odd one, making for strange facial geometrics.

I spotted Josh from across the room and did a slight double take. I had seen him just the day before, but he was noticeably skinnier now, his face sunken, his head looking huge, his smile now so wide it seemed to take up half his face. The day before, he had been all eyes and canine teeth, but at the weigh-in he was all cheekbones, his flesh like wax melted over his bones. He was dressed up in chino shorts and a button-down—everyone else was in joggers and sweats—and he looked profoundly hungry. New valleys caved down into his jawbone and temples, the angles and ratios of his features skewed like a Cubist portrait, forehead and cheekbones taking up more space than my eye expected.

After stripping down to his underwear, stepping on the scale, and having his weight called out—one hundred and forty-six point six pounds, four tenths of a pound under his target—Josh sat down next to his girlfriend, Lara, and opened the cooler of food he had brought with him, visibly delighted with the spread.

I could not imagine the temptation to just tear into it, or his accumulated hunger and thirst. Over the course of the training camp, Josh had lost twenty-three pounds that he hadn't had to spare, and after weeks of calorie restriction, the crescendo of the past week was two days during which he consumed little more than a bit of spinach and eight ounces of water.

When I asked him about the cut and the camp, he told me, "Fighting is traumatic and mentally depleting. It's hard to make decisions. So you have to have enough trust in the person who's coaching you that they know what they're doing and also that they have your best interests at heart. Like, weight cutting? You can die from it. It's very clearly bad for you, and people die from it. You can't just have someone who's like, 'Oh, we'll just put you in the sauna for fucking eight hours and you can't come out until you weigh a hundred and forty-seven pounds.' You have to have someone who wants you to win but also doesn't want you to die doing so."

There is a system of refeeding and rehydrating for fighters, based on largely anecdotal science that doctors won't offer much commentary on because of how dangerous the whole weight cutting enterprise is. After a hard cut, you can't just start guzzling Gatorade on the back end of the weigh-in without risking, at best, severe gastric distress, and at worst, a heart attack or hyponatremia. Some of the fighters go to clinics for intravenous rehydration after their weigh-ins to more safely bring themselves back from the depths of malnourishment and dehydration. The fighters' bodies milling shirtless around the bar might have been strong, but they were also bodies in distress. To deprive a body of food, to force water out of a body, to be repeatedly bludgeoned with fists, elbows, and feet while in such a state: it did not take Josh's testimony or scientific training to understand that these small violences accrue into great trauma, the body like a bucket, collecting them drop by drop and on weigh-in day brimming to the very edge of spilling over.

Josh pulled a packet of organic peanut butter cups out of the cooler, his eyes gleaming. We all watched him slowly start to open the package. Lara's eyes were filled with concern as he told us he had spent the morning sitting in his truck with the heat turned on high and the Arizona sun blazing, trying to eke out a few last ounces of sweat, and while doing so his phone had gotten so hot it shut off and the surface temperature of his sunglasses had burned his skin.

He got the peanut butter cups open, and they were melted. His face crumpled.

Wait

8:00 A.M.

On the morning of the fights, N woke up early to meet Josh for a light workout. I slept in and prepared my materials for the day: notebooks, voice recorder, camera, pens. After spending so much time observing the lead-up to this event, I was nervous about missing something important, some profound or revelatory detail that could slip right past me.

Alone with myself in the quiet of N's absence, I started feeling stupid. Why had I gotten so obsessed with something I wasn't part of? Why wasn't I content to just be a fan, to watch the fights for sport? I had a sense I was trying to edge my way into a vicarious experience—that the violence of Josh's camp and fight was something I wanted to get closer to, as if I was moving closer to a light so that I could see.

2:27 P.M.

I arrived at the venue with N. Josh wasn't scheduled to fight for hours, but there was preparatory stuff—I was still unclear what that entailed—and I wanted to take advantage of the access I'd been afforded, to try to see some small backstage moments. The difference between research and voyeurism was growing less and less clear to me as I worked on this project, and the question of what had drawn me to this particular spectacle was becoming more obtrusive in my own mind, more difficult to leave unanswered.

The air felt tense. I sensed it as soon as N and I rounded the corner of the venue, he carrying a gym bag overflowing with Thai pads and a spit bucket full of gauze and medical tape, I with an iced coffee in one hand and an iced tea in the other. There was a mat set up under a tent in the loading dock. Two fighters lackadaisically shadowboxed and a collection of corner people perched on benches. I followed N to a door into what turned out to be the medical inspection area. Josh was inside. N flashed his corner person's wristband and walked in. I had a wristband too, but it felt intrusive, crowding myself into the tiny room, so I didn't follow him.

Inside the room, a doctor looked over each fighter's HIV and Hepatitis C tests, and checked their vital signs, pupils, and reflexes before declaring them fit to fight. I sat outside waiting for N and Josh to come back out and thought about what I was doing there, what I wanted to see, what truths I had hoped would be revealed. I knew writing about this fight wasn't exactly about sport—I had little in common, as a writer, with the MMA journalists who hovered around the cages at UFC events. What I wanted from this insular world predicated on peril and bravado was to understand something about roughness and to locate myself in proximity to it, a few degrees removed from participation, close enough to see but not feel. This distance from violence was a curious space for me, one that allowed me to obsess over everything about it from the comfort of a chair, a far cry from the ways I had put my own body into the mix when I was younger. Tourism into the lands of violence felt new, but truly it had been a part of everything back then, too.

When I was a teenager I witnessed nightly the wanton pursuit of body damage via sadomasochism and the culture around it, myself intimately involved but separate, always feeling a bit the tourist even as my years as a sex worker stretched into a decade. Later, after the first move in my series of erratic reinventions, when I found myself welding high-rise buildings, I was again immersed in a culture of men, again seeing their bodies in peril. To be a part of that world, I had to slap my own body down on the felt as my buy-in. But still, I was different, and not just for my gender. I ate differently, voted differently, read a different newspaper, had a wholly different set of reasons for being perched on frozen steel in the dead of New York winter, spitting into the wind to watch my saliva harden into tiny shimmering specks of ice on the beam beneath me.

And later, as a writer? Once I had divested myself of the professional pursuit of being tough, once my life fit me in a way no previous iteration had? Even there, I found myself back on the precipice of a space I wanted to worm my way into, a space marked by sweat and danger and camaraderie, of ritual and tradition, of action and proof.

At the venue, I recognized some of the fighters from the weigh-in, and I was stunned by how different they looked after not even twenty-four hours of food and water. Josh's body had regained a bit of its heft and his face looked human again, pinkish and alive where yesterday there had been white and waxy pallor. I wondered, not for the first time, what indefinables had driven him and his cohort of fighters to this place, parched and starving in a parking lot, performing battle rituals from two continents away. Looking around at the stress clearly visible on nearly all the fighters' faces, I wondered what it was they all liked so much about fighting, and what they'd convinced themselves of to arrive at this place.

When I talked to Josh about those questions, he said a lot about a self-testing that is familiar to me. By fighting, he has set up a controlled scenario in which to test his skills and mettle as a person, to demonstrate how powerful he is and expose any cracks that he needs to fill in. That kind of hardness testing is what I was doing on my metalwork crew and at the marathon starting line and in a hundred other places, so I get it. During a fight, he told me, "I have the ability to execute complex plans and immediately react to changing situations under the worst kind of stress. That's everything in a fight. The ability to recognize patterns, knowing when to pull the trigger, when to back away. Being mentally present and focused on the important parts of winning the fight." It was wild to me that he had that much self-awareness, nearly in real time, that it hadn't taken him years of growth and reflection to see his own motivations. For me, that process never happened so quickly.

I know about stories we tell ourselves, and about using the mind to conceal things from the mind, but it had always taken me so much time to figure out what I was up to. Twenty years ago, it had been easy to convince myself that I beat men up for a living because I liked money and power. Ten years ago, it had been easy to convince myself that I walked I-beams because I was tough. But the truths lurking beneath these reductive understandings of what, exactly, a girl with big, sensitive feelings, a girl who grew up in academia, who went to prep school, who aced the SATs and could read a whole book in a single afternoon was doing in these bastions of a certain kind of embodied mindlessness, wherein the purpose of the mind was not to exist for its own sake but to propel the body through sensation? Those truths proved as difficult to suppress as they were inscrutable.

It was hard to explain to myself what I was doing on the outskirts of the fight world, how and why I had located yet another arena of rough culture, why I had again squirmed my way in against its edge. Was it even a valuable exercise to pull apart the ingredients and formulas that make up a magnetic attraction? I felt less driven than pulled, as if I had stopped paddling and just drifted, arriving back at an oddly familiar place, the smell of fear sweat in my nose again, the presence of men weighing heavy against gravity.

I wondered what I was seeking in these spheres of authenticity, the places where no one could talk their way around or out of what would happen, where there was no way to be clever enough or pretty enough to find a loophole. Pain is a great equalizer. Fear, too. We find out who we really are when we face pain and fear, and perhaps I was trying, in my own tentative and vicarious way, to discover who I might really be.

4:00 P.M.

At the pre-fight meeting, the officials went through a long list of rules and requirements: *No knees to the head. No strikes to the spine, groin, or throat. No charging a down fighter. Putting your head down to escape the clinch will cost points. Make sure to have your hand wraps inspected and signed off by an official. If you wear protective headgear, take it off for photographs, but leave your gloves on.* The fighters looked dazed, glazed, and restless, their faces and bodies full of the accumulated weight of all the anticipation that had gone into preparing to fight. I wondered how much information they could reasonably be expected to take in.

"This is when I get nervous," Josh announced after the meeting, dropping his overstuffed bag of gear on the asphalt. He had described this emotional sequence to me weeks ago, and it was unfolding exactly as he had said it would: pure focus and calm during training, full commitment to the weight cut, then a sudden and acute hit of anxiety immediately preceding the fight.

He was second-to-last on the card, which meant there were still hours to sit, wait, and think, and for Josh, thinking about fighting was not a casual act, but an obsessive mental exercise. After unsuccessfully looking for somewhere to lie down he curled up on a concrete bench and rested his head on a metal planter. I felt sure that he was visualizing feints, blocks, kicks, and punches in his head, and I wondered how much of this waiting one man could take.

4:31 P.M.

There was a *lot* of waiting. The interminable feeling of the day's timeline felt heightened by the speed of the past few weeks, in which whole days had seemed to fly by, six weeks out becoming two weeks out becoming ten days out becoming the day before.

Perhaps this stretching and compressing of time is the way of sport itself: delay and anticipation, a perpetual holding pattern, long slow hours punctuated by minutes that hurtle by with gut-twisting speed. Josh described it as "surreal while it's happening, and surreal in retrospect. It just seems like a long blur: boring, boring, boring, punctuated by excitement and terror." This is the way of war, too: what writer Tim O'Brien calls "boredom with a twist, the kind of boredom that caused stomach disorders . . . you'd feel the boredom dripping inside you like a leaky faucet, except it wasn't water, it was a sort of acid, and with each little droplet you'd feel the stuff eating away at important organs."

I wonder what all this waiting and anticipation does to a person—or, maybe, what it does for a person.

5:08 P.M.

N wrapped Josh's hands and I sat close, taking photos and enjoying the particular pleasure of watching someone you love do something they are very good at. The process took a long time—thirty minutes, maybe, longer than the fight itself would last. Josh sat backward on a folding chair with one hand at a time outstretched. N was meticulous, measuring strips of tape and gauze against his own hand, using the flat end of his bandage shears to smooth down the edges of the tape, N's firm hand on Josh's pale wrist, these tiny moments of expertise and care bearing the tenderness that I kept finding just beneath the surface of the fighting life.

"A fighter–coach relationship is a weirdly intimate thing," Josh told me, about him and N. "There's a lot of trust you have to have in someone, to let them coach you to fight. And along with this trust aspect, there's also—any time I've had a friend and we've gone through some shit, maybe both got arrested together, or whatever fucking adventure you went through—every time we fight, that's going on. We prepare together, he's there while I fight, he's there to nurse me back to health. It's a very intimate thing. I think the more you do it, the closer you get."

The fighters' dressing room smelled of menthol rub and anxiety sweat, which wafted out into the air each time someone opened the door. The sun was fading, a vendor was grilling onions, and people were smoking cigarettes around the corner. On his jawline and the side of his head, N had a few grays speckled into his rich black hair. I'd never noticed them before, and I felt so much affection for him when I saw them that it was almost physically painful, a tight fullness in my chest threatening to burst or spill over. As he worked, I watched his profile for so long that I became self-conscious about it, but I still didn't want to look away, tracing his full lips and strong features with my eyes. The feelings I had for him were unfamiliar ones, for me, and they overwhelmed me at unexpected moments, robbing me thoroughly of my ability to act like anything resembling a journalist. I wanted badly to touch him but managed to resist.

Once Josh's wraps were finished and signed off by an official, N explained to me where we would walk when Josh's fight was called. I was nervous to make a mistake, conscious of treating carefully the access that N had afforded me. My only job here was to pay attention and not get in the way, but it was so consuming that I had given myself a stomachache. From so much observing,

I had become all eyes and ears, nearly silent, and I felt deeply stressed when I needed to speak.

N and I had been out until two in the morning the night prior, which was not helping my mental state. Another of his fighters had been defending his championship belt—or, as it turned out, relinquishing it—at a title MMA fight for Combate Américas, another fight league, which is like the UFC for Latin America. The fight was late and the energy in my body had felt weird after watching N's fighter get knocked out in the first round, after sitting in the front row next to the fighter's parents and wife as it happened. The speed of the thing had baffled me. One moment, he was flexing in front of his flag, a dangerous peacock about to charge into battle, and not three minutes later he was done, out, defeated, taking his oversize rhinestone champion's belt and buckling it around his opponent's waist.

No sane fighter walks into a ring or a cage unless he believes he can win, though every fighter must understand, at least in theory, the practical reality that it is possible for him to lose. In any arena in which two people enter and only one can prevail, there must exist a delusional sort of optimism as well as a fatalist acceptance of the possibility of loss, and I wondered how those two convictions can coexist in one fighter, how delicate that balance must be in order to say to oneself, *I know I can win, I believe will win*, in the face of the mathematical certainty that it is just as possible to lose.

It was an odd feeling to witness a loss, to feel the emotional register of a group of people shift so rapidly from hope and excitement to concern and demoralization. There was a whiplash of sorts, as everyone was abruptly extracted from the future and placed uncomfortably in the present, and even though my association to N's fighter was tangential, I had felt the lurch into the reality of a new moment, which had registered as a dullness in my belly, a heaviness in my lower throat. I wondered how the fighter felt, and how much space exists between verbal description and emotional actuality.

I wondered if, for the fighter who loses, a loss was truly, as N said, "a part of the game," accepted as a cost of this bloody business.

6:42 P.M.

About half an hour before his fight, Josh stripped down to his Thai shorts and pulled on his gloves. He looked both powerful and diminished, his swagger intact but his abdominal cavity gaunt. He hit pads with N for a few minutes, loosening up his body, and returned to our staging area with more vigor in his eyes.

"I forgot I'm good at this shit!" he announced, grinning, and stood for N to coat his face with Vaseline, a standard practice that allows punches to slide rather than stick.

It was almost time.

Speed

When it was nearly Josh's turn to fight, I walked with him and N to the backstage area to wait a little bit more. The match before his ended, the emcee announced his name, and suddenly it was happening.

Josh walked up to the ring, N and his other corner person behind him carrying the spit bucket, water, and a rag in case of bleeding. I was supposed to walk with them but I was so frazzled by trying to pay attention and not get in the way that I took a seat on the side, unsure of where I was meant to be. A machine sprayed fog up around Josh's body on cue as the photographer took his photo. His fight song, from *The Lion King*, filled the theater: "I Just Can't Wait to Be King." I wanted so badly to catch every detail that I considered recording the fight, but I suspected that most of what I wanted to inspect and consider was beyond the scope of auditory and visual data.

Josh's opponent was roughly his same height and build: nearly six feet tall, long of limb, carved up with striated musculature. Their two lanky bodies glowed pale under the stage lights, the silk of their Thai shorts glinting. I felt sure Josh would win. Aside from N, I had never seen anyone hit anything as hard as Josh hit things, and so I couldn't reasonably imagine anyone but N dominating him.

In the ring, Josh touched gloves with his opponent, another local fighter who I had seen compete at a Tucson fight night back in December. That night, he had led with his right hand in what is known as an orthodox stance, but tonight, to Josh's surprise, he came out with his left: southpaw.

From my seat directly behind the ring, I could see everything: Josh's body, N's face, the flex of the ropes when Josh got pushed back into them, the collective expressions on the faces in the crowd. I could hear people shouting at him, shouting his name, cheering and demanding and doing that thing that sport crowds do, only more so, because it was his friends and family out there. I wondered if he could hear any of it, if the mental space of the ring had porous boundaries to things like noise and light and sound. I wondered how he felt, right then.

Later, he would tell me, of those moments, "I wasn't scared, but I was lost. Everything was foggy, I couldn't figure out what to do, and I didn't know why." The combination of starvation, dehydration, and exhaustion had left him so cognitively impaired that he could hardly keep track of what was happening: "I was falling apart on the inside."

For all three minutes of the first round, Josh moved his sinewy body around the ring, throwing punches and kicks, but something felt off. I didn't sense the tremendous power and swagger I could always feel misting off him in front of the heavy bag or sparring in the gym; he wasn't moving exactly like himself. But, I thought, an actual fight was necessarily different than practice, and perhaps I just didn't know what that difference looked like?

He traded punches, kicks, and knees with his opponent and landed plenty, neither of them holding the upper hand, at least to my eye. But the meanness of his punches and kicks wasn't quite there, and he didn't dominate the way I had expected him to. He looked a little shook, whether by his own lack of power from the weight cut, by the unexpected left hand of his opponent, or by some other indefinable confluence of factors, I couldn't say, but I saw it in the wideness of his eyes, the missing curl of his lip, a tiny difference in the way he placed his feet on the mat.

I have never been kicked the way Josh was getting kicked. I have been kicked just enough to have the vaguest inkling of how each of the blows he was taking to his legs and body might feel. Before knowing these men, watching them so much, and trying to dabble in what they do, to watch a fight on television or even in person was to grossly misunderstand what was happening on a physiological level. I imagine much of the experience of fighting is impossible to understand without actually stepping into the ring. But my endless questions had afforded me some body knowledge, and I understood that the largely noiseless kicks Josh's opponent was sending into his thighs were causing more pain than most people would offer themselves up for, perhaps more pain than some people will experience in a lifetime.

When the bell clanged to end the round, N jumped into the ring with a stool and Josh sat to breathe and listen. N's face was intense, full of concentration. I had seen him in the corner before with other fighters, and it was a side of him I had not seen in any other space, his usual unflappability replaced with naked will and effort. He leaned close to Josh's face, speaking slowly and clearly, trying to gird him with strategy for the next round.

Each of the next three rounds was a slightly heightened version of the same: Josh looked to me like he was fighting well, but when he landed strikes, they didn't seem to have much effect on the other fighter, who kept kicking him, kicking him, kicking him. There were no decisive blows, and enough reversals of fortune that until the last round I, with my novice eyes, was genuinely unsure who was winning. His opponent got him into the clinch, but he fought out; he got pushed back against the ropes, he fought out. But there wasn't a moment in which I saw the glint of the Josh I had seen in training—the scary Josh, the one who looked like a killer—and by the fifth and final round his leg was visibly red and swollen, his movements had slowed down, and he was spending more time defending himself than advancing.

I knew he hadn't won when the bell rang to end the fight, and he surely did too. He dropped to his hands and knees and let his forehead fall to the mat, whether in obeisance or exhaustion, I couldn't tell. His opponent stood tall next to him, though he, too, was heaving and pouring sweat, and Josh rose to his feet as the judge's decision was announced: the win went to the other fighter, by unanimous decision.

Time shifted again as N helped Josh out of the ring; gone was the interminable anticipatory space of the backstage waiting, gone was the weird fast slowness of the fight itself, which had felt like watching slow moves on fast-forward. Now everything was fast-fast, Josh and N moving off the stage and hobbling to the back area, the doctor coming out to inspect the damage to Josh's wet and limp body, which slid down to the floor, legs splayed out, thigh reddening and filling with fluid even as I stood and watched.

In a few moments, when Josh was cleared to leave and his girl-friend found her way to him, N helped him back up and supported him on the long limp outside, back to the fighters' lounge, depositing him gently in a chair next to the man he had just fought. The pent-up restlessness I had come to think of as emblematic of his character was gone. Fully spent, he sprawled backward, melting into the chair, more tired than anyone who has never done a thing like this could understand.

I carried the spit bucket and tried to help put everyone's belongings back in place. It was dark and a bit chilly, and I had a vague bad feeling that I couldn't place. Josh had already started to reanimate a bit, making jokes with his opponent as they sat and iced their legs together. Their rivalry had lasted only as long as the actual fight, and this was my favorite part to see: the parts that were not on the stage, with the fog and the fight songs and the pageantry of combat. That part was exciting, and I enjoyed the spectacle of it, for certain. But this easy rapport between men who just twenty minutes ago had been spending every ounce of energy they could muster to inflict maximal damage on each other, it transcended common logic. In witnessing such scenes, I understood a little more of what N had told me months ago, about the way fighters can be with each other, the space for affection and respect that is carved out by making a game of violent dominance.

Josh was hurting. I drove him and Lara to the fight's afterparty, and when I offered him a hand to help him out of my truck, he accepted it. He looked like a young bird who had flown through some rough winds, or like a puppy who had tangled too hard with a big dog. Or maybe just like a man who got really skinny and really dehydrated and then got kicked and punched for fifteen minutes without succumbing to exhaustion, fear, or his opponent. He looked tattered, but also fierce, and in that moment I felt overwhelmed with respect for his fighter's heart.

I drove away feeling deeply strange, quiet and full of an unfamiliar swirl of chemicals coursing through my body, though I had done nothing, not really, except sit and watch other people do things. The urge to smoke a cigarette flickered in and I batted it aside, my curiosity about the contents of my state trumping my desire to make it go away.

Distracted, I rolled my truck slowly through a busy four-way intersection. Someone honked and yelled "Bitch," and I very nearly started to cry. I went home, ate some chicken, and fell asleep, and in the morning I still felt it, a strange sensation that had welled up and lodged itself in me somehow. I was embarrassed by this feeling, by my sensitivity, by the likelihood that I was claiming some experience that was not my own. The fighters weren't my people, they were N's. I had just attached myself as a curious researcher and hanger-on, and as a writer I felt duty bound to interrogate my own sense of stakes. But the truth was I felt weird, exhausted beyond what a night of bad sleep could reasonably account for.

I've never been a serious sports fan, but I remember my father's relationship with the Bird-era Boston Celtics: a relationship of adoration and rage, of spittle flying at the television, of an altar boy's reverent gaze and an ogre's bellowing growl. He didn't go to games back then, probably because of the expense, but he watched feverishly as Larry Bird—a man who I know he imagined a bit of himself in—moved into the paint like ballerina, snake, bulldozer, as he swished three after three over the dumbfounded heads of the men who could never quite guard him. I watched my father's feelings during those games, and I watched him afterward, too, and I learned then that you don't have to do something with your own body to feel the reverberations of having seen it.

Steve Almond, in his treatise on violence, fandom, and spectacle *Against Football*, writes, "What kept me hooked was the limbic tingle familiar to any fan, the sense that I was watching an event that mattered. The speed and scale of the game, the noise of the crowd, the grandiloquent narration and caffeinated camera angles—all these signaled a heightened quality of attention." Was that part of why I was there, as much as my grim attraction to the violence? In watching the fights, was I having an experience that mimicked taking a drug? I had noticed, from the first fight N took me to, how time seemed to simultaneously stretch and compress when the fighters were in the cage, the same way it does during experiences of altered consciousness. In my stadium seat I was rooted, alive in my transfixion, fully present in a way I almost never achieve in my daily life, flush like Kerry Howley with Schopenhauer's "sensations fine and fleeting," all details enhanced in a way I hadn't felt since I'd given up my various mind-altering habits.

The next day, Josh and N were on Instagram, posting pictures of Josh's leg—it looked quite bad—and publicly acknowledging the spirit and labor they had each poured into the effort to get ready for the fight.

"Josh did a lot of good and new things, and we made some errors. I am proud as a friend and coach of your performance. We will continue to learn and grow as a team," N wrote.

"The credit for everything I do right is all yours," Josh wrote back. "Thanks for always being in my corner."

A CLEAN, WELL-LIGHTED PLACE

TUCSON, JUNE 2020, 109°
QUARANTINE WEEK 15, GESTATIONAL WEEK 32

After N and I have slowly moved the last of our things to the new house, I go back to the old apartment to clean. I am slow and get tired easily, so this takes two separate days, though the apartment is barely six hundred square feet. I do a better job than is necessary to get our deposit back, scrubbing grout and baseboards in a deep squat and, when my hips get tired of that, on my hands and knees. I do not completely understand why I am dutifully performing this labor, only that it is an act of service I feel compelled to carry out. I clean things I never cleaned when we lived there: the inside back of the oven, behind the fridge, the windowsills under the blinds. I clean so much of our hair, mine long and straight and his thick and curly, that the vacuum cleaner seizes up.

When I am nearly finished and have schlepped our last items down to my truck, I step into our bedroom. The empty space is flooded with sunny light, warm on the blond hardwood, white walls gleaming because I have scrubbed them with vinegar. It is a small, simple room, in a small, simple apartment—the kind of apartment I imagine my parents lived in before I was born, when my dad was in law school and my mom was working at a bank counter to pay both shares of Manhattan rent. The kind of apartment they told me and my siblings about as a sort of cautionary tale of where you have to live if you never make any money. I have been so comfortable here. If not for the baby, I might have stayed indefinitely, paying the cheap rent and not having very much to clean.

The new house is big and rambling, covered in thick-grouted Saltillo tiles and banked by adobe brick walls, a haven for dust and grime, a place that is a real project to keep clean and tidy. I hate cleaning but I cannot relax in an unclean space.

In the empty bedroom, nostalgia rushes into me, and I am suddenly filled with a sort of overwhelm that makes my throat swell in the direction of crying. I think about all the things that have happened here, in this space, mostly in this very room.

N, still new to me, coming inside and sitting down, me thinking that we would have sex and he would leave and it would be whatever, but instead we kissed a little bit and then started talking and I heard myself telling him, in an unvarnished tone, things I usually conceal very carefully. I heard him telling me things men don't often speak of, things people don't usually tell each other. We talked about fear and feelings and alienation and pain, and we did not have sex, and when he left I felt closer to him than I ever had to anyone whose body I had shared.

N, a month or so later, more known but still new, walking through the door right behind me with a small bag in his hand, an overnight bag because he would spend that night with me, our first night together. Me, uncharacteristically nervous, and then not nervous at all, meeting this person who felt less like a stranger than anyone I have ever met before or since.

Us, waking up in this same warm blond light the next morning, both inside the same happiness at the same time, both feeling so human we could not stop grinning at each other.

N, moving underneath me with his hands on the small of my back, breaking the silence of the room to say *I love you*, and me, crying because of how much I believe him, telling him *I've been whispering that to you after you fall asleep for weeks.*

N, moving in with a few small flat boxes and a pair of ski boots and a single bag of clothes.

Me, hurting myself at the gym to the point of crutches, N arranging snacks and water and electronics around my perch on the couch and never once complaining about becoming my caregiver.

Me, nearly a year and a half later, alone early in the morning with a bag full of pregnancy tests, watching lines appear one after another after another, dropping down to my knees and pressing my forehead to the bathroom's tile floor and breathing *Please be real*, then louder, until I was almost yelling, *Please, please, please.* His face when I told him, a few hours later, *I think I'm pregnant*: happy and overwhelmed in equal measure, saying *I know.*

In this apartment we loved each other, took care of each other, made our baby. I feel stupidly sentimental—the apartment is just, after all, a space, a set for a play that is still going on, but I feel feelings rise up and engulf me and I don't have the exact right words for them, happy and excited and nostalgic and grateful, yes, but more too, something woven between.

I run one last pass with the vacuum, press my hands together and do a funny little bow and say *Thank you, house*, lock both doors, and leave.

SICK GAINZ (II)

When I had been living in the desert for a half a year, my body finally fell apart. Years into my compulsive exercise habits, I found myself living between episodes of sickness that left me unable to take a walk, let alone work out. At first, no one noticed, not even me. It happened invisibly. The major systems began to sputter and creak like they do in old and poorly maintained cars: first the transmission, then the gaskets.

The human body has twelve major systems. Seven of mine were in some state of distress or dysfunction: nervous, circulatory, endocrine, cardiovascular, reproductive, lymphatic, digestive. The brakes ground low and the rotors wore smooth. Pieces rusted and bent and fell off. The paint flaked. It was 2019, I was in my thirties, and I had never been sick like this before.

Earlier, when I was younger, my body had broken in contained ways like they all do, piecemeal: a split heel bone here, a torn tendon there, a single kidney shuddering to a halt, strep throat burning as if my gullet were made of hot asphalt, an ovarian cyst blooming to the size a of grapefruit. *You mean an orange?* I remember asking that doctor. *No. A grapefruit.*

It was easy, relatively, to ignore broken, swollen, infected, torn-up pieces when they happened one at a time, but harder to ignore the way my body started collapsing: all of it, systemically dissolving into a chaotic tumble of radiating and pulsing pains, a large web of weaknesses, clammy pieces strung together by what they had in common: they hurt. Once I started getting sick, one of the side effects of all the pain and illness was that it became very difficult to keep track of time, even in retrospect. Time stretched and contracted, time was elastic. Time seized and halted, time was granite.

The first three or five times I was taken down by an episode of sickness, I thought it was the flu, or something similar: something I'd caught, something that had come from outside of me and was temporarily housed in my body, something I could cure with Emergen-C and vitamin B_{12} and hand washing. But it kept happening, kept happening, kept happening. Three months passed that way.

By that time, I had settled, as best as one can, into the scraggy dusty landscape of my life in the desert. I had a big white pickup truck with a tinted windshield and an absurd sun hat and a cache of sunscreen in every bag. I wanted to experience my life—my work, my love, my training at the gym—but even when I was not severely sick, I felt shitty. My baseline had fallen to a place where I was startled on the days I woke up without illness.

At first, I was horrified to discover that I was unable to work out. As the days on my couch stretched, hazy with pain, I would make mental plans for how to stack the whole week's athletic programming into the following week, promising myself that as soon as I felt well again, I would make up the miles or the lifts. Soon, as I learned that I would emerge from the sickness flares weak, sore, and inflamed, those plans became ludicrous even to me, and instead I would retreat into comfort eating, allowing my body to lurch and grind to a halt, all pain and mashed potatoes and my sweaty down comforter. Losing my identity as an athlete in this way crushed me, but bodily emergencies bring with them a reordering of priorities that happens by force, rather than decision. I still trained when I felt well, but it didn't work the same way it always had. Once I knew physicality could be taken away at any moment, it was no longer an expansive space to disassociate into, and it lost the power to organize my life. Had I experienced this loss a different way—the way I did, temporarily, when I broke my heel, say—it might have devastated me. And in a slow, quiet way, it did. But I was busy with a much louder and more frightening loss, feeling my abled body slip away into hazes of helplessness. Knowing that I might never load two hundred pounds on the barbell again was crushing, but not as crushing as knowing there were days when I was unable to drive or walk down the street.

One of the more confounding parts of my mysterious illness was that it was very difficult to describe. I describe things for a living, translating abstract experience into concrete terms. But for my sick body, I didn't have words. I indexed my systems and parts and scoured the internet and tried to pry out phrases or expressions that related to how I was feeling. What I came up with was vague and scant and often nonsensical: *I am sweaty, I am sick/ my skin hurts, my blood is buzzing/everything feels sore, everything feels cold/I've thrown up, I've passed out/my vision is blurry, my heart is beating wrong.*

Three more months passed, and the good days when I felt so well I forgot about my illness stopped happening. I quit making advance plans altogether because of the possibility that I would be too sick to travel or see people. I became so phobic about germs that I didn't want to eat in people's homes. I brought the words *ill* and *unwell* into my daily vocabulary because I was so tired of hearing myself say the word *sick.*

The list of people I was employing to help me maintain a fingernail's grip on my health and sanity grew to alarming proportions. My team was spread across an ocean and a continent. We mostly spoke over email or the phone. If it takes a village to raise a child, it was taking an expensive and highly credentialed battalion to raise this adult. I talked to multiple people about my health on a daily basis. The project of managing chronic illness, I was learning, demands prevention, vigilance, and damage control.

Paul: my nutritionist. He told me what to eat, when to eat, and how much I was permitted to exercise. He remotely monitored my adrenal fatigue and I followed his instructions to a T because he was expensive, nearly six hundred dollars for three months of 24/7 emails and intricate Excel spreadsheets. I could tell him about my crackling joints, my exhaustion, and my insatiable desire for salt, but he didn't close-read my emails. The relationship was so explicitly transactional that I couldn't ignore the truth, which was that I could have stopped emailing him, eaten whatever the fuck I wanted, and CrossFitted myself into organ failure and he likely would never have thought of me again. Maybe, I thought, that would be fine.

Susan: my twelve-step sponsor. She is not a mental health professional, but she has walked her own path and shared her experience to help me decide what to do with my heart and soul and feelings. I told her the worst parts of me in minute detail: the humiliating fears, the unacceptable feelings, the churning resentments. She gave me compassion and hope with stories about how her own life crumbled and how she rebuilt it. Somehow in those conversations I got a better sense of how to shrink my selfishness, my entitlement, my insatiability, and that spiritual progress blunted my ever-growing obsession with thinking about being sick. Being sick and being afraid are hard to disentangle, because it is frightening to develop a mysterious debilitating illness. There was, for me, a loop that developed, wherein I became sick, and then I became frightened of becoming sicker, and then the thinking and the fear made me feel despair, and then the despair and the sickness together made me feel a thing worse than the sickness on its own. When I talked to Susan, I was still sick, and I was still scared, but they weren't all twisted up together.

Dr. Erik: my naturopath. He took my blood, spit, and money and turned them into vague, digressive diagnoses that offered validation and not much more. In the face of so much minimizing from the doctors before and after him, that was worth the cost. He believed I was sick, that my symptoms were real and neither imag-

ined nor somehow manifested by depression or anxiety. He understood without my telling him that I was cold and turned off the
ceiling fan in his office. He told me to run the shower alternately
warm and cool—not hot and cold, that would be too violent—to
create contrast hydrotherapy to soothe my frazzled nervous system. Dr. Erik charged what I perceived to be a premium rate for
administering ozone injections to the chronically ill. *Isn't ozone
poisonous?* I wanted to ask him, but didn't.

N: my lover. He also, at my request, managed my weightlifting programming, athletic injuries, and joint mobility, refusing
to accept any money for these services even though they are his
profession. I continued to try to pay him because I felt so grateful
for his help. He was the only member of my team whose work had
a clear beneficial effect on my body. When I was sick, he took care
of me in our home, but he couldn't fix my days of sweaty dizzy
fevers the same way he fixed my crunchy spine and angry hip
and ripped-up calf. *I'm not a doctor*, he would remind me, gently,
often, usually as I was pressing his hand into some new unidenti-
fied lump I discovered in my breast or my heel or my abdomen.
He would tell me to take a rest day, that it would be okay to eat a
sandwich, that I could relax a little bit. I would tell him I was worried he thought I was crazy, or that I was inventing or manifesting
this illness, and he would look me steadily in the eyes and tell me
he believed me, he understood.

There were strangers, too, many one-time encounters every
month. Early in my illness I begged a doctor at University of Arizona Campus Health for answers about what was wrong with me.
I told her I could feel things swimming in my blood, that I was
regularly too sick to leave my house, that I've always been healthy,

that this was new and alarming and sudden. She typed "general fatigue" on a form and left a message on my online portal saying that there was nothing wrong with me, all my tests were fine. In a doctor's office with a soft chair, a hospital-gauze-covered pillow, and copies of *Architectural Digest*, I paid nearly two hundred dollars to be injected with a drip of vitamins and electrolytes. I went to a laboratory in a strip mall and gave my blood, my urine, my saliva; I went to a medical complex on the edge of town to give scrapings from my vaginal wall, swabbings from my cervix. Influx, outflow, all those needles, all those fluids, all those forms. There was a fury in me, weak but simmering, that built with each of these meetings. Before each new doctor appointment, I girded myself to explain my situation yet again. I waited, tensed, for the interrupting that always happened, for dismissal, or for the prescription or the plastic specimen collection jars or the referral. Sometimes, there would be a brief period of hope followed by more confusion and the mounting worry that I might feel like this forever and no one would ever understand.

Dr. Hines: a doctor of osteopathic medicine. An acquaintance gave me her number in a parking lot and I called without doing any research. It was a rote errand devoid of hope. I had seen so many doctors by then that I expected nothing. In her office, she introduced herself and asked what brought me to the appointment. *I'm sick*, I stammered, flipping the crinkled pages of the legal pad I used to keep track of my symptoms. I was accustomed to being rushed by doctors and so I tried to speak quickly, to only include the most pertinent information, words spilling out of my mouth unpunctuated by breath. She sat quietly and did not interrupt me. Eventually I slowed down. I got to the pages in the pad that I never got to: the small things, the less urgent concerns. After listening to the whole litany, she asked if she could examine me physically. I said yes and she went over my entire body with her hands, spending extra time on my lymph nodes, my reflexes, the soft parts of my abdomen. Her touch was clinical but gentle. It felt good. She praised the fitness of my body and asked me questions about my athletic life, and when she was finished she told me she understood how I was feeling, that I was not crazy, that there was something wrong with me and she didn't yet know what it was but that we would figure it out. The pronoun *we* was new, from a doctor—only N had used it in describing the project of caring for me. I cried so many tears of relief and validation in the office and the lobby that I was afraid her staff talked about me when I left. I took with me orders for a battery of bloodwork. She didn't want to take any guesses without evidence, but she had some ideas. There was a three-month wait for a follow-up appointment.

I was always careful not to call my parents when I was in the midst of an illness flare, though I wanted to, every time. I wanted comfort from them, but it was a mirage. They could only offer anxiety, and their desire to help and to fix me from two thousand miles away was more than I could add to my stack of discomforts. *Go to another doctor,* they would tell me. *We will help you pay for it.* They have trustful certainty in doctors, and they don't understand why I do not. They believe that a doctor can only help, can never hurt, and will always find the right answer. My experience has shown me otherwise. When I was a teenager—depressed, addicted, unmanageable—they sent me to a series of locked wards: hospitals, rehabilitation centers, recovery facilities, detox units, psychiatric institutions, therapeutic boarding school. At each of these places, it was clear to me that I didn't really belong, and that getting out by any means necessary took priority over any kind of treatment or recovery—but that's what every crazy person thinks, right? Two decades later, it feels clear to me that most, if not all, of those lockups were far beyond the level of care I needed, and the privilege of my parents' well-intentioned offers to pay for another kind of specialist always brought to the surface recycled resentments from my younger life, from those years when they didn't know how to help me, from those years when they paid every kind of professional in the tri-state area to recklessly treat me until I was fully institutionalized, medicated to the hilt, and nearly out of my mind.

The difference between acute pain and chronic pain is a semantic one, and also a neurological one. Acute pain is a primary alert system, a message from body to brain that tells us we are presently suffering disease or damage. Though pain is felt, in the loose sense of the word, in the body, it is actually a product of the brain—this is why the pain of phantom limb syndrome (in which amputees experience pain in their missing limb) is, to the sufferer, just as felt and real and agonizing as pain in an existing limb. The feeling appears to come from the meat parts, but really it is coming from the upstairs computer.

Chronic pain differs from acute pain in that it is its own syndrome, functioning similarly in the presence and the absence of disease or damage to the body. Spend enough time in acute pain, and the neurons of your brain will become damaged, causing a chronic experience of pain in the part of the body connected to that section of your neural brain map—even if the body part in question is actually doing just fine. Chronic pain can take many forms: injury, dysfunction, illness. But once it becomes itself—once, that is, the pain of injury, dysfunction, or illness shifts from acute to chronic—then it becomes just one intractable thing: a pain syndrome.

I felt embarrassed when I reread the text messages I sent when I was very ill and in pain. I sent pathetic cries for help to N and to my best friend: people who I knew loved me unconditionally, people who I didn't worry about worrying. *I can't deal with this I feel so claustrophobic in my body I don't know what to do it hurts too much.* That one, sent at 12:42 in the afternoon to N while he was working. There was nothing he could do, and I knew this. But the unfathomability of how much my body hurt felt too big and scary to contain within myself, and as melodramatic as my texts were, they were the unvarnished truth of how I felt. When I was in the sickness, I was no longer *in* pain; I *became* pain. The world shrank to the precise dimensions of my sensory universe. As essayist Elaine Scarry puts it in *The Body in Pain*, her treatise on the cultural and philosophical understanding of physical suffering, "the world was unmade."

Here I feel the need to qualify this amount of complaint with some bona fides. When I was young and a junkie I kicked heroin more times than I can remember. I'd started using heroin to treat the kind of abstract emotional pain that hovers, diffuse and choking. We ascribe that kind of pain to the head or the heart or the soul, and I'd traded it, after a brief period of extravagantly vacant painlessness, for a new kind of pain: the relentless creep of withdrawal sickness. This kind was profoundly physical, felt in the bones and the sinews and the follicles of my hair. Because I was not a very savvy junkie, I kicked heroin without medication and with no money and no cigarettes and no food and an awful thin mattress from Ikea that had sharp parts poking through. I kicked heroin on a couch that wasn't mine, in front of large windows without curtains, without suboxone, without methadone, without clonidine or lorazepam or alcohol or weed or anything. That, then, is my baseline for agony, an experience of physical and mental suffering that I can't fully remember because of the mercy of pain's ephemeral recordkeeping. I know it nearly broke me, but the rest of the details are foggy. All this, nearly a decade and a half before I found myself ill in the desert. All this, my only proof to myself that I am not someone who overreacts, someone who cannot handle pain, someone who collapses under small pressure.

A decade and a half later, I was grown and mostly sane. And the truth is that, compared to junkie sickness, the illness that my body lapsed into was not as bad. Not compared to sitting across a table, glassy eyed with the incoming tide of withdrawal sickness, staring into the receding hairline of one of my sex work clients with what I hoped passed for interest, trying to do the math on how fast I could get the cash and if I could get to the spot before it closed for the night. Not compared to the way I used to sink into my wide-wale corduroy loveseat that was too short to stretch out on to face the inevitable when I had exhausted all my other options. Some girls, they tricked when they were sick. This was—still is— unimaginable to me. When I was a junkie, withdrawal sickness leveled me in a way that did not allow me to so much as cross my apartment, let alone perform the arrangement-making and physicality of earning that kind of money. I only tricked ahead of time. That sickness took a toll on me in a way nothing before or since did, and eventually, after holding my hand on the burner for long enough, I said, *okay, I'm scared now.* That was what changed me—not the desire for a different life, or the distaste for tossing bits of my body around for fixed rates. That part of the addict's life? I could have kept doing that shit forever. It was the pain that stopped me. The sickness.

And so in my thirties, employed by an R-1 university, with health insurance and a driver's license and my teeth fixed, I was baffled at how I arrived back at a version of the same sharp precipice, balancing between fear of and for my body. I hadn't been a junkie or a wreck for a long time, but still there was something deeply wrong with how I took care of myself. I slept and ate and exercised in ways that raised peoples' eyebrows. Sometimes I was doing too much, sometimes too little. Sometimes what felt normal and correct to me looked like a disorder to others. I was genuinely unclear about what was good and what was bad, what was care and what was abuse, what was discipline and what was punishment. The part of me that was always seeking, with the certainty of poor judgment, the easier, softer way? That part will kill me quickly.

That part loves heroin booted slow into the thick veins at the crooks of my elbows, loves a man who grabs the fleshy part of my upper arm hard enough to leave pale violet fingerprints behind, loves fistfuls of semolina bread dragged through room-temperature butter and vomited as fast and violently as it was swallowed. I knew I must manage the clamors of that part. I had to quiet them down from an aggressive demand into a soft cry into a whisper low enough to call an auditory hallucination, the echo of another time and place. I did this managing with contrary action: running shoes pulled onto sore feet; barbells hoisted overhead on trembling shoulders; coffee slurped, black, into my hungry belly; three alarm clocks, bleating, early. This management of habits was the most important of all the protocols, because without it the gobbling would happen, a relentless gobbling of everything: food, drink, sensation, experience, all of yours, his too, *is there more, I need more, always more.*

When I got sick, I lost track of everything. My work, my appearance, nutrition, hydration, voicemails, emails, text messages, appointments: they all receded. The world, unmade, shrank to the small confines of my fever, of my night sweats, day sweats, soggy sheets, of my pain and the words for it: *thumping, coursing, brewing, simmering, crushing*: words for trying to destroy a thing or cook a thing, not just trying to exist in a body. When I came out of those episodes, it felt like a tide rolling back to release me from its brackish cloak. I felt oddly unchanged by the experiences. The only lessons I took with me were for how to better prepare for the next time: prep some food to keep in the freezer, make sure I have a heating pad on hand. I wanted to have some kind of revelatory epiphany about the nature of my existence, about precarity and gratitude and entitlement, but in truth I was usually so spent that it was all I could do to claw myself back into the driver's seat of my life, catch up on emails, and go to the grocery store.

During the hottest part of the first summer I was sick, I was meant to get on a plane to New York at eight in the morning. I had been up until eleven the night before. It was too late and I had known it, but *it's okay*, I told myself, *I will sleep on the plane.* I stayed up giggling, watching a bad movie and having good sex, feeling so excellent that I could not recall how it might be to feel bad. I could not, during the joy of those moments, remember how I had felt the last time I had been sick, when I was alone in a truly wretched motel room in New Mexico that I had purchased in the middle of a drive for the sole purpose of having a place to be unexpectedly sick. That time, I was scared, feeling my body crumple like a sad damp rag so fast I could watch it happen, one hour my eyes feeling starchy and my neck starting to throb, a few later, a sweaty mess on the bathroom floor, vomiting out of my nose and whimpering like a child, unclear what had happened, my vision blurry, too sick to drive home. But more than a month had passed since then, and even though that episodic routine had happened more times than I had counted in the surrounding six months, each time worse and faster and more perplexing, and even though no doctor could explain to me what was glitching in my body, what was falling apart or not sparking or coming unglued in there, I knew in the deep and certain place that something was wrong, something was different, something was coming for me.

Since the episode in New Mexico, I had taken meticulous care of myself, measuring ozone-filtered water and carefully deskinned breasts of organic free-range birds into glass containers, careful about toxicities, careful about imbalances, careful careful careful. I had taken great care.

A month later, when the sickness came for me again, it took less than two hours. Eleven at night, falling gently to sleep on N's chest, utterly well and happy enough to split open with it. One in the morning, waking in a cold sweat to waves of pain rolling in and out of my body, my neck a bright epicenter of sharp pain, my stomach confused and sour. *I think I'm sick*, I whispered, after lying there for a while thinking I must be wrong, that it must be the ceiling fan or the blanket or not enough sleep or I forgot to have enough water or my protein powder could have been expired or any other not-exactly-water-tight theory. N's hand was on my forehead as soon as I said it; he sleeps like the parent he is, never fully gone, always available for emergency. *You feel warm.*

By three in the morning I was in too much pain to lie down or stand up or sit, I could only lurch fitfully from one end of my couch to the other, chewing on the corner of a pillow and whimpering like a kicked dog. I hated myself in these dramas of weakness. Where was my stoicism, where was the person who ran a hundred miles on a broken heel, where was the person who mistook a kidney stone for a rough day at the gym?

I was far too ill to get on my flight, or even to call and cancel it. I stayed on my couch for nearly a week. N brought me soups and noodles and ginger drinks and bubbly water that went tepid on the table. He made me smoothies with hidden greens and rubbed my sore neck and never once said *Why don't you get up?* or *Are you sure it's that bad?* As I waited for something like that—some revelation of impatience and disgust—I realized it was my mother's voice I was waiting for. *Get up. Don't waste the day. Up and at 'em.* Those, my mother's mantras. I didn't understand when I was young that she was working her own stuff out—that she had grown up in the mushroom cloud of her own mother's depression, and that to see someone horizontal in the middle of the day, sick or not, was so triggering to her own fear of depression and immobility that it really felt to her like an act of love when she dismissed my need for rest and compassion. I didn't understand until she eventually got ill herself—until she lost months of her life to a catatonic depression that culminated in a psychiatric hospitalization, the ultimate enforced rest—that she was outrunning something of her own, something she might not have had a name for but that had been perched on her shoulder for her entire life. I'd thought it was all about me.

As an adult, no one snapped at me that way anymore, not since Dean. Not for sleeping, not for resting, not for being sick. I didn't sleep much anymore, anyway. Seven hours was a good night, most were closer to five. When I rested I felt guilty, lazy, self-indulgent. I felt my mother's panicky impatience and my father's gritty judgment, vestiges of my childhood when no one understood the difference between depression and sloth. To be sick, even, felt shiftless and indolent. I curled into myself on my sectional couch and wondered *What would I do if I didn't have a home? What would I do if I was in the military? What would I do if I had kids?* I asked myself those questions as a way to cast my genuine immobility as something slothful, something I had afforded myself, something I didn't deserve.

As I pursued answers for what was wrong with me, I wanted to go back to the beginning of the life of my body and ask some questions. I wanted an accounting. What was administered, what was collected. A reckoning. I wanted, too, to go back to the beginning of the life of my mother's body and ask the same questions: what was taken, what was given. My best friend's mother had relentless sugar cravings during her pregnancy, she ate pancakes every day during the gestational period. A poet, she wrote my friend a letter describing this habit and telling her which pancakes of what variety she ate on which days. I have such complicated feelings about how care was wielded in my childhood, so many notes on how I would prefer things had been handled. Once I became troublesome, my mother dragged me into the offices of doctor after doctor to be inspected, injected, examined, dosed. My mother, who I feel sure didn't get as much care as she wanted or needed, inadvertently poisoned me with care.

At a twelve-step meeting I once heard a young woman share about her mother's Munchausen-by-proxy syndrome, about being maliciously dosed with amphetamines and then marched into cardiac units, about deception and coercion and lies. I know my mother is not in the same universe. I know that the ways she damaged me were obtuse at worst. And still. I have to live in this body.

My parents believe in western medicine like it is religion. When I was a child and a teenager, my mother took me to doctor after doctor and let them fill my young sad body with barely-FDA-approved drugs, nearly every '90s-era antidepressant and mood stabilizer that I know of, plus more, in wild combinations for off-label uses. My mother loved me and wanted me to be well. I felt poisoned by all these third-party ministrations, addled to this day in ways I will never fully understand or unravel. I love my mother, and I am grateful for her love. All of those things are true at the same time and my body is the stress point of their dissonance.

The doctor's office does not feel like a safe place to me. It was the first place I was taught to discard my instincts, the first place

I was told to ignore my discomfort with being touched. My first doctor, a man. Why do people take their small daughters to male doctors? Why must the indoctrination into grimacing under big cold clammy hands begin so soon? That doctor was fine, I think, and what that means is he didn't try to fuck me, or anything similar, which is a pretty low bar to set, but still. He was probably kindly and avuncular, I don't remember, and why not afford him the benefit of the doubt. But I do remember recoiling from his touch. I remember dreading the crumply paper and thick Naugahyde of the examination table, the too-bright lights, the clinical smells. I hated everything about it, but I had to go, and there, the first lesson: *This body is not yours, not really. You don't get to decide what happens to it, where it goes or who sees or touches it.* The bodily autonomy of small children feels personal to me, too personal, perhaps.

It never made sense to me that it was supposed to be bad to sell touch, because I was taught, like everyone else, to give it away so easily, against my own desire. My mother takes pills in narrow plastic jars the color of traffic cones and sunglass lenses melted together. My mother takes pills I got sent to rehab for taking.

At rehab, any pretense of bodily autonomy was relinquished. You are inmate as much as patient—any sense of being a "client" vanishes when you are compelled to sit as your belongings are meticulously sifted through. At rehab, they were better at inspecting than the TSA, but still, they missed things. At rehab you might have your cavities searched. At rehab you must open your mouth for inspection.

The mental hospital, however, was worse. When I was fifteen, years before my unmanageability had even reached its apex, I was walked into the upper-floor unit of an old hospital in Rockland County, with bars on the windows and plexiglass protecting the nursing staff from the patient population: from us. When you are fifteen you lack the legal authority to leave such a place; you remain locked in until a team of people, including your parents, makes a group decision that you should be released. The sound of the adolescent unit's door locking noisily behind me, laminated ELOPEMENT RISK sign fluttering against painted steel, is the precise sound of my parents' betrayal. At that hospital you were not permitted to shave your legs unless a staff member was staring directly at you: *one-to-one*, they called it. At that hospital you had to report your bowel movements—*I had a BM*—and if you didn't you would be given Colace to aid your stubborn digestion and if you didn't take the Colace it would be forcibly administered. At that hospital, if you didn't eat for long enough your small frail body would be held down by three large male staff members while a fourth threaded a length of aquarium tubing up your nose, ripping tearing pushing burning through your septum, down your trachea, into your esophagus, down into your belly. At that hospital, if you ripped the tube out in the middle of the night, spurting hot red blood all over the institutional linens, they would get a new tube and jam it back in, past your abraded nasal passages, into your stubborn cavities. Things they fed us at that hospital: pound cake, ranch dressing in individual serving pouches, cigarettes, Prozac, Ensure.

Unlike my mother, I am scared of pills, of shots, of medicine, of care, but I didn't know what else to believe in, where to go with my hurting parts and broken systems. I, too, believe in the redemptive power of the diagnosis, of the medical professional. I wanted a doctor to fix me, but I was also terrified of the things they had done to me in the name of treatment. I wanted to scream every time I was offered a flu shot, which I was irrationally afraid of even though I strongly believe in vaccines. After so much bad doctoring and damaging pharmaceuticals, I experience genuine panic at the thought of any foreign substance entering my body. I feel myself leaving logic behind with the urge to scream at every receptionist, doctor, and nurse who tries to press a shot on me that I DON'T WANT TO BE SHOT UP WITH INFLUENZA, that my health is precarious, that you fuckers did this to me in the first place with all your miracle drugs and fast fixes, you broke me worse than I was to begin with and I am now too fragile and too tough—that's right, *both*—to succumb to the fucking flu.

In the desert, I drove myself into a state of baseline anxiety from wondering. I wondered if the UV index was making me sick, if I had caught Valley Fever from inhaling fungus that leaked out of the hard-packed Arizona ground, if I was ill from adrenal fatigue, if there were mold spores in my HVAC, if I was somatizing some kind of panic disorder, if drinking bubbly water out of cans had leached heavy metals into my blood. I wondered if I had touched or breathed or swallowed something toxic, if I had moved my body in some incorrect way or amount, if I had neglected to consume something vital. I wondered, often, if I was crazy. In the desert I had more questions and theories than I did answers, and for so long that it felt settled into a permanent state, I stayed sick.

Dr. Hines called me to her office one afternoon when I was limping sullenly around my apartment. I had been sick, off and on, for most of the year. I didn't feel very well and I had hurt my leg at the gym and it was hot and I was all out of the hope that used to spring from my sternum when someone offered me a new hypothesis on what might be wrong with me.

At her office, she sat me down in a small examining room, produced a sheaf of papers in a manila folder, and pulled up a chair to face me, turning her back on the computer. I was feeling miserable and I wanted her to hug me. I suspect she would have if I had asked, but she did me one better: she looked me in the eye and said, without a hint of uncertainty, *I have the results of your bloodwork and I know why you have been so sick.*

I was too stunned to respond. No one had ever spoken to me about my sickness so clearly and surely. She spent nearly forty minutes with me, going slowly through each of the papers in the folder, explaining what each level and value indicated, and at the end told me that I have an endocrine system disorder, and that the systems of the body are interconnected—that it's not like plumbing and electrical, snaking through separate depths of a structure, it's like a circuit board, each surge and charge of electricity affecting not only the resistors and capacitators that it surges through and into, but each other element of the system as well. She showed me on the papers where my endocrine system indicated imbalance, where my ability to process blood glucose was faulty, where my reproductive system was failing to function. She explained androgens and insulin and luteinizing hormone and anovulation. She told me that these constellations of glitches were why I was never able to become pregnant. She told me they were why I felt so sick, why the sickness was so unpredictable. She told me there were treatments.

I left the office with a prescription for pills I was both afraid
of and desperately grateful for: pills that would arrest one of the
specific glitches in my endocrine system, and that, if they worked,
would cause a cascade of corrections throughout the rest of my
body's systems, until everything fell into balance. I would know
they were working, Dr. Hines told me, if I stopped getting sick.

I didn't go to the pharmacy to fill the prescription for a week.
When I finally went to retrieve the pills, the pharmacist stressed
the severity of their main side effect: extreme gastric distress, not
dangerous but very uncomfortable. I nodded my head and he said,
again, with more emphasis, *It may be very bad.* I took the crin-
kly paper bag out of his hand with a nod of thanks and trudged
back to my truck, already feeling defeated. This was always the
way: trading one set of pains for another, trying to play the cards
in a way that improved the hand I was dealt, trying to manip-
ulate my body to be more comfortable to live in. I didn't want
extreme gastric distress, and I didn't want my endocrine system
to keep misfiring me into bed-bound illness. I had only a shred of
hope that the pills would work at all, and I wanted new cards: a
fresh body, mint condition, unmarred and undamaged, without
the traces of ten years of street drugs and fifteen years of dodgy
pharmaceutical interventions. I wanted cells that would do cell
things and neurons that would do neuron things and I wanted to
not have to think about any of it. I wanted this body to run like
an efficient factory, for all the systems to flawlessly execute their
intended purpose, and its insistence on instead squelching along
like a wet engine confounded me, infuriated me, crushed me with
its inescapability. I don't *live in* this body; I *am* this body. It is less
a carapace than the substance of my soul.

In the morning I swallowed one of the small white pills with a few bites of food. I waited for the extreme nausea I was promised, for my belly to start gurgling in distress, but nothing happened. The next day, same thing. I felt fine, blank, even. I wondered if the pills were fake, placebos for a crazy woman. I looked up their stamp and appearance on an online pharma database. They looked right. I still felt fine. I took another one the next morning, with just a cup of black coffee, feeling its chalky friction against the sides of my throat, and I waited.

One of the truths about complex chronic illness is that there are no neat answers, no final diagnoses, no simple treatments. I didn't know that yet when Dr. Hines told me she could fix my problem, and I desperately wanted to believe her, so I did. In a way, she wasn't wrong. It's just that I had a lot of problems, and they were all built out of and on top of each other. I was sick. I wasn't ovulating. I couldn't get pregnant.

She fixed the last two with the small white pills, so quickly that I still think of her as something of a wizard. And in fixing them, the baby-size hole in my heart was able to be filled. The rest—the ever-looming flares of sickness, the body that was consuming itself, the constant encroachment of pain—was for later.

A BODY THAT'S BEEN TROUBLED

TUCSON, JULY 2020, 111°

QUARANTINE WEEK 18, GESTATIONAL WEEK 35

Since becoming pregnant, I now think about labor nearly every time I engage with my body as an animal. Eating, having sex, using the bathroom, washing myself in the shower; as I touch and use my mammalian parts, I think about how I will use them during labor, and how they will be altered by it.

As my pregnancy progresses, my body looks less and less the way it did, and it isn't just that it's bigger. My flesh is softer, my meat parts feeling less like meat and more like pudding, yielding easily to the pressure of my fingers even under flexed tension. The large muscles of my thighs and calves and arms—quadriceps, sartorius, and iliopsoas, gastrocnemius and soleus, biceps, brachialis, triceps, and anconeus—are no longer visibly delineated from each other; where I used to be a collection of discrete parts I am now just one thing: body.

These changes, though distinctly unaesthetic to my eye, bother me less than I would have expected. I think a lot about why. Some of it is outside me, probably: I feel with N, for the first time in my life, the security of a love that is not based solely or mostly on the way my body looks or feels or what it does. The precarity that feels embedded in a love that I cannot maintain simply by making sure I remain hot shook me, at first—and sometimes it still does, which is a truth that is hard to know and to say. But it holds me, too, this love that can easily weather the shifting and changing of a body, this love that lives somewhere between and within our bodies but is made of something smokier and more capable of living everywhere, in the voids and the shallows, the bones and sinews, the curve of a smile and the vibration of a whisper. I don't feel very sexy and I do feel very loved. Nothing about the coexistence of those truths conforms to the logic of the world as I had understood it before N. But it is true and real and it endures, so I am forced to consider and adjust that understanding, to amend what I believed to be firm truths.

The movements of our baby inside my body change every few days or weeks. First it was barely perceptible flutters that I second guessed, not sure they weren't just the movements of my own digestion. To feel something in myself that both is and is not myself is eerie and awesome. There is something alien within me and of me, therefore, I too am alien. We two aliens, existing together in one body, as close to one as two humans can possibly be. I stand in genuine awe of my body and its hidden capacity for miracle. A few weeks later, it was a distinct fluttering. I knew it was our baby, but I could only feel them if I was still and quiet and paying attention. Then, for a while, it was soft jabby moves that I imagined to be small punches and kicks, coming from all points in my abdomen, sometimes pressing out of me, sometimes in, sometimes addressing my bladder or intestines, sometimes pushing toward my navel. I could feel the movements with my hand and sometimes see them at the skin of my belly. Eight months into my pregnancy, our baby is making slower, stronger, swirly moves and also staccato tapping, late in the night and early in the morning and randomly throughout the day. I am brought to gasping by the newness of the feeling as I lie on the couch listening to the sound of the water in N's shower. I want him to feel every movement, to keep his hand pressed to my belly at all times like I do. I want him close to me in a way that I recognize as excessive and perhaps codependent, and most days I can gently laugh at these feelings.

The feeling began in December, when I was pregnant but didn't yet know it, when we had just started trying to conceive a baby but hadn't fathomed that it could happen so quickly. I knew my body felt different and I hadn't bled in a long time but I also thought I knew, from my doctor, that I would not be able to get pregnant without some combination of pills and needles and procedures, that we would not be able to be together, sweaty and wanting in our bed, that we would have to be together via a plastic specimen cup and several trips to a cold clinic where the office would smell like chemicals and someone who is not N would jam tools inside of me with cold laboratory jelly, that they would give me a paper towel to wipe off with and I would go home feeling sticky and defeated—and that's if everything went well.

I was in Hawai'i in December, alone, wanting to surf and see friends but feeling oddly exhausted and antisocial, spending a few of my days lazing in bed long past the morning time when the wind is calm and the water is glassy, *wasting my time*, as it seemed. I stayed this way for a week and then I missed N so much that had I not been too embarrassed I would have flown back to Tucson immediately, back to a place that suddenly and clearly was home, back to him. I wanted something amorphous that I could only articulate through details: to touch his hair, to smell his neck, to snuggle my back into his front on our big crumb-covered couch, to kneel in front of him and swallow him, to make him a Mason jar of coffee and press it into his hand on his way out the door. None of those desires seemed important enough to leave what had previously been my home and favorite place in the world, at last-minute-ticket-change expense, and so I stayed, aching for him and wondering at my clinginess, wondering if I had tipped over into some precipice of dependence, wondering what it all meant as my stomach swirled with a nausea that I explained, variously, as vitamins on an empty stomach, dodgy Chinese food, too much raw fish, seasickness, jet lag, anxiety, improper workout fueling, heat exhaustion, dehydration, car sickness, and the flu.

Later, it would make more sense. But when I got home and even that didn't feel close enough, it was still confusing. I wanted to be with N in a way that felt unbounded, and I feared in myself an unquenchable thirst, an unfillable hole, some kind of psychological damage I thought I'd resolved rising up to make things weird. I wanted to crawl into his lap and bury my head in his neck at all times of all days. I found it increasingly difficult to be with him in public without incessantly touching him. He would go to work and I would spend the days waiting until I could see him again, feeling like a puppy left at home all day, slobbery and wanting, so needy that even my shame at this state couldn't make me hide it. I wondered if I was losing it, if some of the calm and security I always felt with him had slipped into the slime of my own neuroses, if Dean had been right after all: that I am insatiable, *a bottomless pit of need.*

I was horrified by this development, and I tried to hide the extent of it even as I tried to tell N truths about how I felt: *I need more time with you, I miss when we had days together, I want it to be just us today.* It felt like he was receding, even though he was steadily loving and warm and desirous of me, even though he kissed me on the mouth every morning and every night and many times in between, even though he spent his scant spare minutes with me, even though, even though. *I miss you,* I kept thinking, as he sat right next to me. I wanted to crawl into his skin.

And then one morning I knew. I didn't want to let myself think it, because I feared somehow it would vanish, but out of the many feelings I felt when I finally took the first of the twelve pregnancy tests I would go on to administer in quick succession, lining up the positive sticks on the floor of our tiny bathroom as proof I am human and alive and more miraculous a creature than I had given myself credit for, surprise was not one of them.

Now it all makes sense: my suddenly strange body, my frightening need. It is easier to explain the shifting and deepening of my love for N with biology; I feel less responsible for it that way. If the hormones that are allowing our baby to grow are also making me want to Velcro myself to him and never be apart, that is not some fault of my improper personal evolution or some crack in the foundation of my autonomous personhood. I am just an animal, doing an animal thing, clinging now to this other animal who is irrevocably doing this animal thing with me, who is now forever a part of me, and I of him, two animals bigger than dumb ideas about how to keep a man or stay desirable in your thirties or *keep the magic alive.* The magic is here, in this biology so miraculous and mundane, in this home place that lives now in a person, in the smell of his neck and the touch of his hands and the way I, once a broken animal, am well and whole again.

I am ready for pain, like every animal is, whether they know it or not. I am ready to scream and tear and bellow and rend, and I am ready too to heal and breathe and sigh and rest. I am ready for all of it, every joy and horror, everything known and unknown, every thing that can happen. It has taken a long time to get here. I have suffered far more than was necessary. There were so many easier ways to arrive.

And yet. I regret nothing. I would cash back not one of the tears or lost moments that have deposited me here, none of them, the worst and the best inextricable from each other, this home place the center of a labyrinth that was very difficult, nearly impossible, to arrive at, but that is true and real and will house these animals, safely, sparing us not from pain but from numbness, sparing us nothing of the truths of these bodies, letting us love.

EPILOGUE

TUCSON, SEPTEMBER 2020, 104°
QUARANTINE WEEK 26, GESTATIONAL WEEK 43

Acknowledgments

Thank you to everyone who helped me write this book. I would not have been able to start or finish it without your support. I am forever humbled by your generosity, candor, and love.

For mentorship, reading, coaching, notes, edits, and talks: Melissa Febos, Alison Deming, Ander Monson, Chris Cokinos, Kat Ivanov, Maddie Norris, Lucy Kirkman, Natalie Lima, Emma Thomason, Hea-Ream Lee, Julie Lunde, Kate Beutner, Shawna Yang Ryan, Cindy Franklin, Rachel Reeves.

For telling me to keep writing: Hap Veeser, Vicki Whicker, Andrew Devitt, Kate Bernheimer, Katy Nishimoto, Dahlia Heyman.

For love, friendship, truth, and helping me believe in myself: Nicolas Holck, Claire Steines, May Conley, Matt Flego, Susan and Stacie May.

For walls, quiet, chats, and a surrogate home space: Corky Poster, Mary Goethals, and Pima.

For opening your life and training to my research: Josh Purcell

For believing in this book and reading it the way I hoped it could be read: Matt McGowan, Drew Weitman.

For the funding and creative guidance that allowed me to get started: the MFA program at the University of Arizona.

For my brains, for support of every kind, and in gratitude for agreeing to skip over all the previous pages: my parents.